LITTLE BOOK OF
SHERLOCK HOLMES

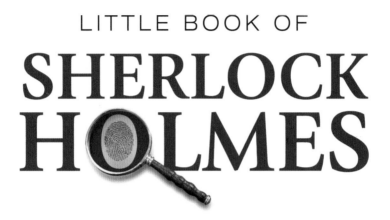

Michelle Brachet

LITTLE BOOK OF

SHERLOCK HOLMES

First published in the UK in 2014

© Demand Media Limited 2014

www.demand-media.co.uk

Printed and bound in Europe

ISBN 978-1-909768-52-9

Contents

Introduction

Sir Arthur Conan Doyle was born on 22nd May 1859 and lived until 7th July 1930. He was a Scottish physician and writer who is most remembered for his creation of Sherlock Holmes, the best-known fictional detective and the epitome of scientific thinking.

In 1886 Conan Doyle wrote *A Study in Scarlet*. This novel, which was published in *Beeton's Christmas Annual* in 1887, was revolutionary and was to be the introduction to the world of the immortal Sherlock Holmes and Dr. Watson.

In 1902 Doyle was knighted by King Edward VII for services rendered to the Crown during the Boer War and was appointed a Deputy-Lieutenant of Surrey.

Conan is not part of his surname but is only one of his two middle names.

His full name is Sir Arthur Ignatius Conan Doyle. He began using Conan as part of his surname after graduating from high school. When studying at the University of Edinburgh, Doyle was friends and fellow classmates with Robert Louis Stevenson and Bram Stoker.

He had a varied and interesting life involving many pursuits. It was reported that he bought a car without ever having driven one before, and became one of the first motorists in Britain. In 1911, he participated in the Prince Henry Tour, an international road competition to challenge British cars against German ones. He was on the same cricket team as the Scottish writer Sir James Matthew Barrie and they also collaborated on a comic opera called *Jane Annie*.

He played as a goalkeeper for amateur

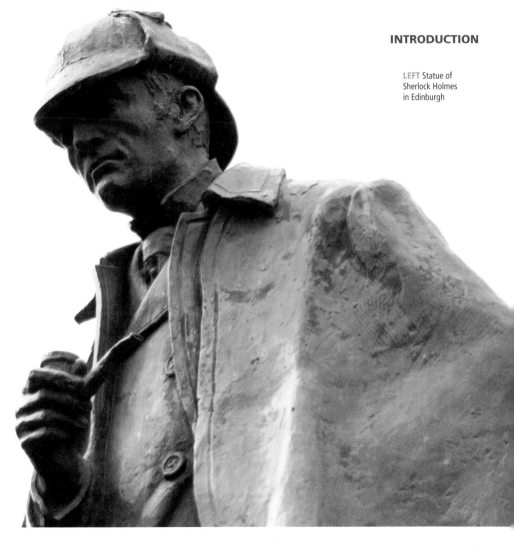

LEFT Statue of
Sherlock Holmes
in Edinburgh

> " *The character Sherlock Holmes, created by Sir Arthur Conan Doyle, is a fictional detective whose ability to adopt many disguises, his use of forensic science, and his shrewd logical reasoning to solve difficult cases made him famous.* "

side Portsmouth Association Football Club under the pseudonym AC Smith. In addition to liking cricket and football, he was enthusiastic about skiing and helped to popularise it. After moving to Davros in Switzerland in 1893, he mastered the basics with the help of two local brothers, Johann and Tobias Branger. Together they crossed the Maienfelder Furka from Davos. It is also thought that Doyle was the first Englishman to document the excitement and thrill of skiing. Doyle correctly forecast that in the future many Englishmen would visit Switzerland for the skiing season.

Doyle ran for parliament first in Edinburgh in 1900 and then in the Border Burghs in 1906. He enjoyed respectable support on both occasions but was not elected. When he couldn't become a soldier in the Boer War because he was overweight, he volunteered as a ship's doctor and sailed to Africa instead.

Sherlock Holmes was not Doyle's own favourite character. In fact he actually killed him off in 1893 in a story titled *The Adventure of the Final Problem* but he relaunched the character ten years later due to public demand and monetary pressures.

There is a square in Switzerland now named Conan Doyle Place and a statue of Sir Arthur Conan Doyle can be found at Crowborough Cross in Crowborough where he lived for twenty-three years.

The character Sherlock Holmes, created by Sir Arthur Conan Doyle, is a fictional detective whose ability to adopt many disguises, his use of forensic science, and his shrewd logical reasoning to solve difficult cases made him famous. Holmes and his fictional friend Doctor John H. Watson lived at 221B Baker Street, London from 1881 to 1904. Holmes featured prominently in four novels and fifty-six short stories. The first novel in 1887 was *A Study in Scarlet;* the second in 1890 was *The Sign of the Four.*

When the first series of short stories appeared in *The Strand Magazine,* beginning with *A Scandal in Bohemia* in 1891, the character's popularity increased tremendously. Two novels and further short stories were published covering the period 1880 to 1914.

The literary character of Sherlock Holmes was inspired by men Conan Doyle had been taught by, or studied with, at Edinburgh University. Based mainly on Doctor Joseph Bell, a lecturer at the medical school of the University of Edinburgh, Bell was noted for making a diagnosis from the smallest observations and he also assisted in a number of police investigations. Sir Henry Littlejohn was a Scottish surgeon, forensic scientist and public health pioneer. Chairman of Medical Jurisprudence at the University of Edinburgh Medical School, he made a large impression on Doyle, and it is thought, provided an inspiration for Holmes. Littlejohn served as Police Surgeon and Medical Officer of Health of Edinburgh, highlighting for Doyle a link between the detection of crime, forensics and medical investigation.

Professor James Moriarty is the archenemy of Sherlock Holmes in the fictional stories written by Sir Arthur Conan Doyle. Moriarty's character is a criminal mastermind who is described by Holmes as the 'Napoleon of Crime'. The character of Moriarty was introduced predominantly as a narrative contrivance to enable Conan Doyle to kill off Sherlock Holmes. He featured directly in only two of the Sherlock Holmes stories. However, in more recent uninspired work, Holmes acknowledged that he had been proven to be the most dangerous of all criminals and he has been given more importance as primary adversary. Moriarty fell to his death in the short story *The Adventure of the Final Problem.*

John H. Watson, known as Dr. Watson, is a fictional character in the Sherlock Holmes stories. Watson was an English physician, formerly in the British Army and was Sherlock Holmes' friend, sometime flatmate and assistant. Doyle realised the necessity of having someone to whom the detective can make perplexing remarks, and be acquainted with the case, without being in on the conclusions drawn from them until the appropriate time. It is acknowledged that any character who carries out these functions in a mystery story has come to be known as a 'Watson'.

In 1988 a statue of Sherlock Holmes was placed in Conan Doyle Place in Switzerland and a statue of him has been erected in Picardy Place, Edinburgh, where Doyle was born.

Sir Arthur Conan Doyle

HIS EARLY LIFE

Arthur Ignatius Conan Doyle's birth took place on 22nd May 1859 at Picardy Place, Edinburgh, Scotland. The Doyles were an affluent family who were well known in the art world. His father, Charles Altmont Doyle, was the only unsuccessful member of the family. Charles was a civil servant who suffered from chronic alcoholism and epilepsy. He was born in England of Irish Catholic descent and died in an asylum in 1893.

His mother, Mary (Foley) Doyle, a lively, educated young woman, was Irish Catholic and ran a boarding house. She was passionate about books and was a brilliant storyteller, making stories come alive. This made a big impact on the young Conan Doyle. His parents married in 1855 but in 1864, due to Charles's increasing addiction to alcohol, the family were temporarily separated and scattered around Edinburgh. In 1867 the family were reunited but were forced to live in shabby, dirty flats at 3 Sciennes Place.

When Arthur was nine years old, his wealthy uncles agreed to pay for his education. He was sent to the Jesuit preparatory school at Hodder Place, Stoneyhurst, a Roman Catholic school, which he attended from 1868 to 1870. He then went to Stoneyhurst College until 1875. Arthur hated the intolerance relating to his studies and fought against corporal punishment that was widespread in most schools at that time.

SIR
ARTHUR
CONAN DOYLE
AUTHOR
1859–1930
WORKED
AND WROTE HERE
IN 1891
ARTHUR CONAN DOYLE SOCIETY

During these very unhappy years at boarding school, Arthur found enjoyment when he practised sports, especially cricket, which he was very good at. He found great happiness and solace when he wrote to his mother and it became a ritual that he continued to do this for the rest of her life. He also became aware that he enjoyed storytelling and had a natural talent for it. He often entertained the younger students with his amazing stories. From 1875 to 1876 he attended the Stella Matutina Jesuit school in Feldkirch, Austria, but later in life he rejected religion and became an agnostic.

Arthur Doyle graduated in 1876 aged seventeen. He had a natural sense of humour and great sportmanship and in spite of his early years, was ready to make the most of his life and pursue a career. He was anxious to make amends for his father's failings and to be successful for his mother's sake.

Although the family's tradition was in the world of art, Arthur decided to follow a medical career and from 1876 to 1881 studied medicine at the University of Edinburgh Medical School. He was influenced in this direction by Doctor Bryan Charles Waller, a lodger his mother had taken in. Doctor Waller had trained and carried out his medical studies at the University of Edinburgh.

As a young medical student Arthur met Robert Louis Stevenson and James Matthew Barrie, both future authors who were attending the university. One of his teachers, Doctor Joseph Bell, made a big impression on him and influenced his future. Doctor Bell was an expert at observation, deduction, logic and diagnosis. Sherlock Holmes, the fictional detective later created by Conan Doyle, exhibited these same qualities.

During this time Conan Doyle also worked for a while in Aston, Sheffield, as well as in Shropshire and during his studies he started to write short stories. His first, named *The Haunted Grange of Goresthorpe* was unsuccessful, but his first published story on 6th September 1879, *The Mystery of Sasassa Valley* appeared in Chambers' Edinburgh Journal. He went on to have his first non-fiction article, *Gelsemium as a Poison,* published in the British Medical Journal on 20th September of the same year.

In 1880 he wrote a story called *The Surgeon of Gaster Fell,* which could have provided an insight into circumstances around the detention of his father in a lunatic asylum. Also in 1880 Conan

> *" Many years later he accepted that the Arctic had awakened a born wanderer in him. "*

Doyle was employed as a doctor on the 'Hope of Peterhead', a Greenland whaler leaving for the Arctic Circle. The ship first stopped near the shores of Greenland where a seal hunt began. Conan Doyle did not enjoy the brutality involved but was fascinated by a subsequent whale hunt. He very much enjoyed the camaraderie on board the ship and acknowledged the change in himself from a youth to a well-grown man. Many years later he accepted that the Arctic had awakened a born wanderer in him. His first tale about the sea called *Captain of the Pole-Star* included the adventure that he participated in.

Conan Doyle reluctantly returned to his studies in the autumn of 1880 but after the Arctic trip, he changed from being a struggling student to becoming a ladies man and he often boasted about being in love with many women at the same time.

He graduated from university in 1881 after gaining his 'Bachelor of Medicine and Master of Surgery' degree. His sense of humour led him to drawing a sketch of himself receiving his diploma with a caption that read: 'Licensed to Kill'. He became a ship's surgeon on the steamer SS Mayumba, which was on a voyage from Liverpool to the West African coast. He disliked Africa immensely and gave up his position as soon as the boat returned to England.

For a short, difficult period, he spent time in Plymouth with George Turnavine Budd, a former classmate who became his partner. Forty years later he wrote about this episode in *The Stark Munro Letters*. By this time Conan Doyle was on the verge of bankruptcy and left to move to Portsmouth to open his first medical practice at 1 Bush Villas in Elm Grove, Southsea. Due to lack of funds, however, his rented house was sparse with only two rooms furnished that his patients would see. The remainder of the house was left almost empty. The practice was slow to progress, but he worked hard and compassionately for three years before his practice became successful and earned him a secure income. Conan Doyle completed his doctorate in 1885 on the subject of tabes dorsalis (loss of movement in the spinal column).

HIS NAME

Doyle is often referred to as 'Conan Doyle' but it is uncertain whether this was his surname. He was baptised with the Christian names 'Arthur Ignatius Conan', and 'Doyle' as his surname. These names appear in the register of St. Mary's Cathedral in Edinburgh. However, after graduating from high school he started to use 'Conan' as a surname. In reality his last name is just 'Doyle'. He was knighted as 'Doyle' but when he married his second wife, she was known as 'Jean Conan Doyle'. Michael Conan is recorded as being his godfather.

DOYLE'S WRITING CAREER

During this time in his life, Conan Doyle divided his life between being a good doctor and writing stories with the intention of becoming a recognised author.

He wrote the novel, *The Mystery of Cloomber*, which was published in 1888 and which illustrated Doyle's fascination and interest in the paranormal and spiritualism. He wrote many short stories including *The Captain of the Pole-Star* and *J. Habakuk Jephson's Statement*, which were based on his experiences at sea. This last work helped to make popular the mystery of Conan Doyle's fictional *Marie Celeste*. The actual name of the deserted Canadian-built, American owned, merchant brigantine was Mary Celeste.

Doyle had great difficulty finding a publisher for his works. *A Study in Scarlet,* his first notable piece, was published in November 1886 by Ward Lock & Co. and he was paid only £25 for all the rights to the story. It appeared in *Beeton's Christmas Annual*, *The Scotsman* and the *Glasgow Herald*, and was well received. This was the story that featured for the first time, the characters of Sherlock Holmes and Doctor Watson.

It is thought that the character of Sherlock Holmes was inspired by Joseph Bell, one of Doyle's university teachers whose powers of deduction and observation were very similar to those of Sherlock Holmes. Robert Louis Stevenson recognised the similarities and wrote to Conan Doyle complimenting him on his written adventures and ask-

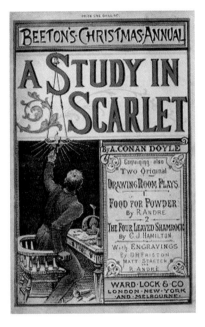

Doyle felt that he was being exploited by the publishers, so he parted company with them.

In 1891, Conan Doyle was writing short stories featuring Sherlock Holmes, when he became dangerously ill with a serious attack of influenza. For several days his life hung in the balance. When he recovered and was well again, he realised that he had been foolish in attempting to combine a medical career and a literary one. He therefore made the difficult choice to abandon his medical career, but he was delighted with his decision.

Doyle began to write for *The Strand* from his home at 2 Upper Wimpole Street and his short stories about Sherlock Holmes were published in *The Strand Magazine*. At about this time, he was also collaborating with James Matthew Barrie on the libretto of the opera, *Jane Annie*.

The historical novel which Conan Doyle most enjoyed writing was *The White Company*. The main characters possessed the same attributes of honour and integrity that the author had experienced during his life. An unfinished work and surviving work called *Narrative of John Smith* was not published until 2011.

LEFT Cover of Beeton's Christmas Annual for 1887, featuring A. Conan Doyle's story A Study in Scarlet

ing whether it was his old friend Joe Bell.

In 1890 *The Sign of the Four* was commissioned as a sequel to *A Study in Scarlet* by the Ward Lock Company and it subsequently appeared in *Lippincott's Magazine*. This work was to be influential in establishing Arthur Conan Doyle and Sherlock Holmes in the history of literature. However, as a new author,

A LOVE OF SPORT

Conan Doyle was an enthusiastic sportsman who had sampled most British sports. He played for Portsmouth Association Football Club, an amateur team, as goalkeeper under the pseudonym A. C. Smith.

Doyle's love of cricket started in his school days and he played throughout his life. As a committed cricketer, he took part in ten first-class matches for the Marylebone Cricket Club between 1899 and 1907. In 1902 he scored forty-three against London County. This was to be his highest-ever score. He sometimes bowled and once took the wicket of the famous William Gilbert 'W. G.' Grace. He also enthused about boxing, including participating in a late night match, which took place while he was still dressed in his formal evening clothes.

Doyle was also an ardent golfer who, in 1910, was elected captain of the Crowborough Beacon Golf Club in East Sussex for that year. He played off a respectable handicap of ten.

ABOVE Marylebone Cricket Club Logo

RIGHT Sir Arthur Conan Doyle and his family

HIS FAMILY

During his younger years his mother had regaled him in stories of chivalry and righteousness, which stayed with him and guided him throughout his life. It was these principles that surfaced in 1885 when, as a practising doctor, he invited the Hawkins family to move into his home. The family had been threatened with eviction from their rented home due to Jack Hawkins suffering from seizures. Jack, a young member of the family suffered from cerebral meningitis, a serious and terminal illness.

This arrangement meant that Jack could become a patient and the family could stay together. Unfortunately, Jack was so very ill that he lived for only a short time. It was during this period that Louise, Jack's sister, became impressed with the young doctor. She admired his dedication and kindness and Conan Doyle was impressed with her charm and gentle ways. They soon fell in love and were married in August 1885.

The marriage was amiable and pleasurable and they had two children. In January 1889, a daughter was born

SIR ARTHUR CONAN DOYLE

SIR ARTHUR CONAN DOYLE

named Mary Louise and two years later, a son they named Arthur Alleyne Kingsley, known as Kingsley. This was to be the most significant event of their life together.

After studying Ophthalmology in Vienna, Conan Doyle moved to London in 1890. He lived at Montague Place and then moved to South Norwood. He set up an Ophthalmology practice at 2 Devonshire Place, but he did not see a single patient. This gave him the opportunity to concentrate on his writing.

Conan Doyle was leading a very busy life but he was not aware that his wife was sick with tuberculosis. When this was diagnosed she was expected to live for just a few months, but with his great care and treatment she was kept alive for many more years than expected.

In 1893 Conan Doyle's father died in the Crichton Royal in Dumfries. Doyle was working hard at his writing while caring for his wife, but the death of his father added to his troubles and it resulted in him becoming depressed. He spent more time investigating and being fascinated by spiritualism and he became a member of the Society for Psychical Research, which seemed to be a declaration of belief in the occult.

He was offered, and accepted, to give a series of lectures in the United States. In September 1894, his brother Innes sailed with him to New York. After giving talks and lectures in over thirty cities, the tour was deemed a great success. According to an article in the *Ladies' Home Journal*, he was extremely popular and made many friends during his visit. He returned to England and *The Strand Magazine* published the first of the *Brigadier Gerard* stories, which was very well received by the readers.

During the winter of 1896, Conan Doyle decided to take his wife Louise on a trip to Egypt where he hoped the warmer weather would help her condition. While there, he wrote a novel named *The Tragedy of the Korosko*. Although Conan Doyle, a virtuous man of high principles, remained celibate while his wife was alive, in 1897 he fell in love with Jean Leckie. She was a beautiful and successful woman. Aged twenty-four she was a trained mezzo-soprano, a sportswoman and an academic.

In order to make money during this time, Conan Doyle wrote a play about Sherlock Holmes. William Gillette, an American actor, read the script and asked for Doyle's permission to make

SIR ARTHUR CONAN DOYLE

changes to it. Conan Doyle had no objection so the revisions were carried out. There was little left of the original work when it was returned to him. However, the play made a very successful tour in the United States and was equally lauded in London when it opened at the Lyceum Theatre in 1901.

Conan Doyle volunteered to fight when the Boer War started. Due to weight problems at the age of forty, however, he was not fit enough to be enlisted. He immediately volunteered as a medical doctor and in February 1900 he sailed to Africa where he worked in the Langman Field Hospital at Bloemfontein. During the few months that he spent there he had to fight battles against germs and viruses. To his horror he found that there were more medical staff and soldiers dying from typhoid fever than from wounds of war.

Conan Doyle's wife Mary Louise died in July 1906 and in September 1907 he married Jean Elizabeth Leckie. He took his new wife and his two children to a new home called Windlesham Manor in Sussex. It was a lovely house and he lived there for the rest of his life as well as keeping a flat in London. Between 1909 and 1912 they had three children named

Denis Percy Stewart, Adrian Malcolm and Jean Lena Annette.

Sir Arthur and Lady Conan Doyle sailed to New York in May of 1914, but Doyle was disappointed that the city had changed so much since his last visit, twenty years earlier. However, the couple then travelled to Canada where they stayed for a short time and they found it delightful. They returned home a month later, mainly due to Conan Doyle's concerns of an impending war with Germany.

When war broke out, Conan Doyle again tried to enlist with the army.

By this time he was fifty-five years old and was once again denied enlistment. He proceeded to set up a civilian unit consisting of more than a hundred volunteers and suggested to the War Office that they could provide body armour to protect troops and inflatable lifeboats and rubber belts.

Winston Churchill wrote back to him, thanking him for his ideas.

THE 'DEATH' OF SHERLOCK HOLMES

In 1891, Conan Doyle wrote to his mother with his thoughts of slaying Sherlock Holmes, telling her that he was taking his mind from better things. He wanted to stop writing about his famous detective and concentrate on more serious literary works to get his career back on track. His mother, and others tried to stop him, but ignoring all protestations including his mother's, Conan Doyle decided to be rid of Sherlock Holmes. When he and his wife had toured Switzerland, he had found the exact spot where he wanted Sherlock Holmes to meet his end.

In 1893, *The Final Problem* was published, in which Sherlock Holmes and his archenemy Professor Moriarty apparently fell to their deaths together down The Reichenbach Falls in Switzerland following a hand-to-hand struggle. Conan Doyle tried to placate his readers by allowing Holmes to go in a blaze of glory, ridding the world of a dangerous criminal. Conan Doyle was happy to be free of his medical career and free from the fictional character he had created but who, in his opinion, was overshadowing his finer work.

There was, however, public outcry at the demise of Sherlock Holmes and after some time his fans persuaded Conan Doyle to bring him back. He did this in the novel *The Hound of the Baskervilles* in 1901, despite this being set

BELOW
Reichenbach Falls

before The Reichenbach Falls incident. The success of the novel did in fact lead to Holmes's long-term comeback, much to the delight of his fans.

Sherlock Holmes was revived in *The Adventure of the Empty House* published in 1903, the story of which was set in 1894. This was Doyle's first Holmes short story in ten years. It explained that only Moriarty had fallen, not both men, but as Holmes had many dangerous enemies, it was opportune for him to be thought to have died. Very few people knew that Sherlock Holmes was still alive, having beaten Moriarty in the struggle at The Reichenbach Falls, and watching him plunge to his death. He decided that there were sufficient holes in eyewitness statements for it to be credible to resurrect Holmes. *The Adventure of the Empty House* marked the beginning of the second set of stories, which Doyle continued to write until 1927.

The period from 1891 to 1894 in Doyle's literature is the period between Holmes's disappearance and presumed death and his reappearance in the aforementioned story. This period is referred to as the 'Great Hiatus' to Holmes scholars and aficionados.

POLITICS

In 1900, after the Boer War, there was worldwide criticism of the United Kingdom's conduct. Conan Doyle wrote *The War in South Africa: Its Cause and Conduct*. This work, which was widely translated, defended and justified the United Kingdom's part in the Boer War. Later, Doyle thought that this work was responsible for him being knighted by King Edward VII and his appointment as a Deputy-Lieutenant of Surrey. In October 1900 he wrote *The Great Boer War*, a journal, which was a great literary work of military study. In addition to being a report of the war, it was a high-level commentary relating to some of the organisational failures of the British forces.

After the Boer War and when he returned to England, Conan Doyle was ready for a new direction in his life. He turned his attention and his energy to politics, running for a seat in Parliament as a Liberal Unionist for Central Edinburgh. He narrowly lost the election, however, so returned to London and to his writing.

He was inspired to write *The Hounds*

by King Edward VII. In addition to services rendered to the Crown during the Boer War, it is thought that the King, being a Sherlock Holmes fan, wished to encourage him to write more stories. In 1903 *The Strand Magazine* began to publish *The Return of Sherlock Holmes* in regular instalments.

During this period, Conan Doyle was leading a very active life. He was caring for his wife Louise, seeing his new love Jean Leckie, playing golf, flying in early airplanes and hot-air balloons and driving fast cars. Although he was enjoying this hectic life he was not really contented. What was missing from his life was his prolonged yearning for public service, so he made another attempt at politics. He stood for a seat in Parliament again as a Liberal Unionist for Hawick Burghs. In spite of receiving respectable support, he was still not elected.

The campaign for the reform of the Congo Free State, led by diplomat Roger Casement and journalist Edmund Dene Morel came to Conan Doyle's attention

of the Baskervilles in 1901 after spending a period of time in the Devonshire moors where he had visited the famous Dartmoor prison during his stay. While writing this novel, he realised that he needed a hero, but instead of inventing a new character, he decided to use Sherlock Holmes. As he did not want to resurrect the detective, he wrote the story as an earlier, untold adventure. When published, the novel became a sensation across the world.

In 1902, Conan Doyle was knighted

and he became a supporter. He was a man of high morals who could not tolerate injustice. In 1909 he wrote a leaflet called *The Crime of the Congo,* in which he condemned the hideousness of that colony.

After becoming an acquaintance of Morel, Casement, and Bertram Fletcher Robinson, it is thought that they influenced several characters in the novel *The Lost World*, which was published in 1912. Doyle ended his friendship with Morel and Casement, however, when Morel joined and helped to lead the pacifist movement during the First World War. However, Doyle did try unsuccessfully to save him from facing the death penalty when he was found guilty of treason against the Crown during the Easter Rebellion.

ADDRESSING INJUSTICE

Conan Doyle was a passionate champion of justice and after personally investigating two closed cases, his work led to two men being cleared of the crimes of which they were accused.

The first case concerned a man named George Edalji, a half-British, half-Indian lawyer. In 1906 he was accused of writing menacing letters and maiming animals in Great Wyrley in the Midlands. The police were convinced of Edalji's guilt, even though the maiming of animals continued after the accused was in prison.

Conan Doyle contacted Scotland Yard to report a case of miscarriage of justice. He had detected that Edalji's eyesight was so bad that it was proof that he was incapable of carrying out the dreadful deeds. He was liberated.

To a certain extent this case assisted in the establishment of the 'Court of Criminal Appeal' in 1907. His work also helped to provide a way to put right other breakdowns of justice.

In 1908 Conan Doyle came across the second case involving a German Jew named Oscar Slater. He was a gambling-den operator who was convicted of battering an eighty-two-year-old woman in Glasgow. Doyle became involved because he highlighted many inconsistencies in the prosecution case and he had a strong feeling that Slater was not guilty. He paid most of the costs of Slater's appeal, which was successful. In 1912, Doyle wrote *The Case of Oscar Slater,* which provides a detailed account of the event.

SPIRITUALISM

The war that Conan Doyle had foreseen, World War I, had dreadful consequences for him. His son Kingsley died from pneumonia after being wounded during the Battle of the Somme in 1916. His brother Innes, his two brothers-in-law and two nephews also died just after the war. This caused Doyle to sink into deep depression and to find comfort from spiritualism and its efforts to prove existence beyond the grave. He became a member of The Ghost Club, a well-known supernatural organisation and he retreated into an imaginary world of spiritualism and the existence of fairies.

He became deeply involved with the occult and wrote continually about spiritualism. His wife came to accept his beliefs and to share his intense enthusiasm, developing an aptitude for trance writing. After 1918, Doyle found little time to write fiction as his involvement into the occult deepened. The family, including their three children, accompanied Conan Doyle and his wife on psychic crusades to America, Australia and Africa.

Doyle's fascination for fairies was enhanced when he came across some photographs taken by a Yorkshire family. They appeared to depict tiny fairies dancing around two young girls. Doyle believed the photographs to be genuine and in 1922 wrote *The Coming of the Fairies* in which he included the photographs with beliefs about the existence of fairies and spirits. This book, however, caused harm to his reputation and great disappointment to his fans. Many years later, the teenage girls that were featured, admitted that they had faked the photographs.

In 1926 Doyle wrote *The History of Spiritualism,* which played tribute to the perceptions and telepathy of spiritual bodies created by Eusapia Palladino and Mina Crandon. For a short time Doyle became friends with the American magician, Harry Houdini. Houdini was convinced that spiritualist mediums were frauds and used trickery. Doyle would not be convinced and even thought that Houdini possessed supernatural powers himself. Houdini called his feats 'illusions'. Doyle wrote about this in *The Edge of the Unknown.* Their disagreements on this subject caused their friendship to come to a bitter end.

ABOVE Houdini and the ghost of Abraham Lincoln, c. 1920-1930. Houdini demonstrates how a photographer could produce fraudulent "spirit photographs" that documented the apparition and social interaction of the dead

During the 1920s, Joseph McCabe, a sceptic of spiritualism, published claims that Doyle had been duped by mediumship trickery. William Hope and other fraudulent spiritualists were exposed, which made Doyle lead a mass resignation of members of the Society for Physical Research. They were under the impression that the Society was against spiritualism. Doyle and another spiritualist William Thomas Stead, were duped into believing in telepathy, until Julius and Agnes Zancig admitted that their mind reading act was a trick and gave details of the method used.

Richard Milner, an American historian of science, believed that Doyle might have been responsible for the hoax of 1912, the Piltdown Man. A fake hominid fossil was created that deceived the scientific world for more than forty years. It is thought that *The Lost World* includes various clues pointing to an involvement in the hoax. In 1974 Samuel Rosenberg wrote *Naked is the Best Disguise,* which claimed that in his literary work, Doyle left obvious clues with regard to the repressed and stifled facets of his mentality. Conan Doyle claimed to have spoken with the spirits of many famous men; he believed that he had conversed with Cecil Rhodes, Earl Haig and others.

After a few years, and having spent a large amount of money chasing his dreams, Doyle was forced to write again. He wrote a novel of psychic experiences named *The Land of Mist,* which was followed by *The Disintegration Machine* and *When the World Screamed.* In 1928, he wrote *The Casebook of Sherlock Holmes,* which was a collection of his last twelve stories about the escapades of the immortal detective. In his later years Sir Arthur conveyed his wish that he should be remembered, not for his novels, but for his psychic work. His son, Adrian Conan Doyle, made it known that the whole family believed he would continue to communicate with them from the spirit world.

DEATH

Ignoring the fact that he was suffering from a painful heart condition, Conan Doyle decided in the autumn of 1929 to go on a psychic tour to Holland, Norway, Sweden and Denmark. On his return, he was suffering so much pain that he had to be carried ashore. He remained bedridden at his home at Windlesham Manor, until 7th July 1930, when at the age of seventy-one and surrounded by his family, he died of a heart attack. Lady Doyle had cared for him throughout his illness and he died peacefully. His last words were spoken to his wife, when he whispered, "You are wonderful". Lady Doyle died in London in June 1940.

Following his death there was some argument about his place of burial. He was not a Christian but considered himself to be a spiritualist. As such, he was buried in the Windlesham rose garden on 11th July 1930. Some time later he was moved to be buried with his wife in the churchyard in Minstead, in the New Forest, Hampshire.

BELOW Sir Arthur Doyle's grave at Minstead, England

Chapter 2

The Character of Sherlock Holmes

Sherlock Holmes is one of the most important characters in literature. He is one of only a handful of characters in which people actually believe to be real. Part of this is simply the weight of history, but it is also because he is one of the most complex and flawed characters in literary history. As the central character in four novels and fifty-six short stories, he has remained part of society for well over a hundred years and shows no sign of becoming dated or disappearing.

The prototype for the modern mastermind detective, Holmes first appeared in Conan Doyle's *A Study in Scarlet*, published in *Beeton's Christmas Annual* of 1887. He then made his second appearance in *The Sign of the Four*, which was published in *Lippincott's Monthly Magazine* in 1890. By the time the first series of short stories were published in *The Strand Magazine* in 1891, beginning with *A Scandal in Bohemia*, the character of Sherlock Holmes had already grown enormously in popularity.

As the world's first and only 'consulting detective', Holmes pursued criminals throughout Victorian and Edwardian London, the south of England, and continental Europe. Although the fictional detective had been anticipated by Edgar Allan Poe's C. Auguste Dupin and Émile Gaboriau's Monsieur Lecoq, Holmes made a singular impact upon the popular imagination and has ever since been the most enduring character of detective fiction.

Throughout the four novels and

221b

SHERLOCK
HOLMES

CONSULTING DETECTIVE

1881-1904

THE CHARACTER OF SHERLOCK HOLMES

fifty-six short stories featuring Holmes, a number of characters recur, including the bumbling Scotland Yard Inspector Lestrade; the group of 'street Arabs' known as the Baker Street Irregulars, who are routinely employed by Holmes as informers; his even wiser but less ambitious brother, Mycroft; and, most notably, his formidable opponent, Professor James Moriarty, whom Holmes considers the "Napoleon of crime."

Of course, in addition to Holmes himself, there is also his friend and biographer Dr. John H. Watson, who narrates all but four Sherlock Holmes stories. Holmes himself narrates *The Blanched Soldier and The Lion's Mane* and *The Mazarin Stone* and *His Last Bow* are written in the third person. Dr. Watson is very much a part of Holmes's professional life and they lived together for two periods of Watson's life: before his marriage in 1887 and then again after his wife's death. Watson's actual role in Holmes's life is predominantly twofold. As well as being the detective's right-hand man in terms of being his accomplice, messenger and assistant with regard to conducting and solving cases, he is also Holmes's chronicler or "Boswell" as the detective refers to him.

The relationship between Holmes and Watson is an extremely close one and is the most significant one throughout his life. Holmes is, however, often critical of Watson's writings, often viewing them as too sensationalist rather than just concentrating on the pure "science" of his craft. For example, he comments on Watson's writing, 'Detection is, or ought to be, an exact science and should be treated in the same cold and unemotional manner. You have attempted to tinge it with romanticism, which produces much the same effect as if you worked a love story ...'

Holmes's affection and fondness for Watson, although mostly hidden beneath his somewhat cool and intellectual exterior, occasionally comes to the surface. For example, in *The Adventure of the Three Garridebs*, Watson sustains a superficial bullet wound during a confrontation with a villain. Holmes's reaction to the incident is somewhat moving for Watson as Holmes says, 'It was worth a wound; it was worth many wounds; to know the depth of loyalty and love which lay behind that cold mask. The clear, hard eyes were dimmed for a moment, and the firm lips were shaking. For the one and only

time I caught a glimpse of a great heart as well as of a great brain. All my years of humble but single-minded service culminated in that moment of revelation.'

Holmes offers some insight into his detective methods,

ABOVE Sherlock Holmes, Dr. Watson and Mycroft Holmes in *The Adventure of the Greek Interpreter*

claiming that "When you have excluded the impossible, whatever remains, however improbable, must be the truth." His detecting abilities become clear, though no less amazing, when explained by

his companion, Dr. John H. Watson, who recounts the criminal cases they jointly pursue. Although Holmes rebuffs praise, declaring his abilities to be "elementary," the oft-quoted phrase "Elementary, my dear Watson" never actually appears in Conan Doyle's writings. What Holmes does often say with regard to his logical conclusions is that they are "elementary", meaning that he thinks them to be both obvious and simple. He also refers to his friend Watson occasionally as "my dear Watson", but never did Conan Doyle combine the two phrases. Although not spoken by Sherlock Holmes, the phrase "Elementary, my dear fellow, quite elementary", does appear in P.G. Wodehouse's 1910 novel *Psmith in the City*. It is therefore quite clear how, over time, the famous Sherlock Holmes phrase that didn't actually ever exist morphs into something that is wrongly quoted worldwide and has been for many years!

In Conan Doyle's original stories, very little details are given away about Holmes's life outside of his work recorded by Watson and many scholars have spent many years picking through what evidence there is to try and put some kind of biographical picture of Holmes's early life and extended family together.

It is thought that Holmes was born in 1854 due to the fact that in the story *His Last Bow* Holmes is described as being sixty years of age and the story was set in August 1914. Throughout the Sherlock Holmes stories there is not a single mention about his parents and Holmes merely refers to his ancestors as having been "country squires". The only two family members that are present are his great-uncle Vernet – a French artist - who is mentioned in *The Adventure of the Greek Interpreter* and his brother Mycroft. Mycroft has a more regular and enduring role through Doyle's Sherlock Holmes literature and a somewhat detailed picture about Holmes's brother can be put together. He is seven years older than Holmes and is a government official with a unique position in the civil service. Mycroft appears in *The Adventure of the Greek Interpreter*, *The Final Problem*, *The Adventure of the Bruce-Partington Plans*, and is mentioned in *The Empty House*. Mycroft is in fact portrayed as being even more gifted in the craft of observation and detection than Holmes, but due to his lack of drive and energy, which his brother has in abundance, he never surpasses

Holmes, preferring to spend his time in "a club for the most un-clubbable men in London", the Diogenes Club.

Watson's narrations describe Holmes as a very complex and moody character who, although of strict habit, is considerably untidy. He describes Holmes as "bohemian" in both habits and lifestyle and as eccentric, having no regard for contemporary standards of modern levels of tidiness. In *The Musgrave Ritual* (1893) Watson describes Holmes: 'Although in his methods of thought he was the neatest and most methodical of mankind ... [he] keeps his cigars in the coal-scuttle, his tobacco in the toe end of a Persian slipper, and his unanswered correspondence transfixed by a jack-knife into the very centre of his wooden mantelpiece ... He had a horror of destroying documents ... Thus month after

BELOW Sherlock Holmes in *The Adventure of the Musgrave Ritual*, which appeared in The Strand Magazine in May, 1893

month his papers accumulated, until every corner of the room was stacked with bundles of manuscript which were on no account to be burned, and which could not be put away save by their owner.'

His housekeeper, Mrs. Hudson, looks after his London residence at 221B Baker Street, but she never interferes with Holmes's paperwork as he, throughout the stories, often digs through his mess of papers and artifacts from which he finds exactly what he was looking for, regardless of the mess.

Holmes appears to undergo bouts of mania and depression throughout his life, the latter of which are accompanied by pipe smoking, violin playing, and cocaine use. Interestingly, Watson does not, however, regard Holmes's smoking habits as a vice, although he never partakes himself and occasionally berates Holmes for creating a "poisonous atmosphere" with his tobacco smoke. Having written a monograph on the ways and wherefores of identifying tobacco-ash residues, Holmes's smoking habits provided a useful detection method.

Holmes is most famous for smoking tobacco in his pipe, but he also on occasion smoked both cigars and cigarettes. In addition to this he was a habitual cocaine user and an occasional user of morphine, both of which were in fact legal drugs in England during the late nineteenth century; this habit was fairly commonplace during this period. Injecting his cocaine with a syringe that he kept in a special Moroccan leather case, Holmes believed that the drug stimulated his brain and he would often take it when he didn't have any exhilarating cases to think about or solve. Watson, however, did not approve of Holmes's cocaine habit and referred to it as his "only vice". Regardless of the fact that in *The Adventure of the Missing Three-Quarter* Watson claims to have "weaned" Holmes off cocaine, his doctor friend regards the lack of Holmes's drug taking habit as "not dead, but merely sleeping".

Although Watson is portrayed as the more virtuous of the two, he equally does not seem to mind or condemn situations in which Holmes is prepared to break the law on behalf of a client, or bend the truth if he views it as morally justifiable when solving cases however. Holmes is a patriot through and through, and in a number of stories acting on behalf of the government, is intent on protecting the nation. In *His*

Last Bow, which is set at the beginning of World War I, he also carries out some counter-intelligence work.

Holmes's characteristics can arguably border on being one of arrogance, but then on the other hand he is not a seeker of fame and often allows others, the police for example, to take credit for the work that he has done. He does, however, get immense pleasure from coming up with deductions that are far superior to those of the police, often baffling them at the same time. Holmes's character is often cold and seemingly dispassionate, however on occasion, and most notably when in the middle of a particular adventure, his character can also portray an astonishing sparkle of passion.

Holmes is such a well-known detective, thanks to Watson's stories plus newspaper articles, that clients often go direct to Holmes first with a case, either working alongside the police or bypassing them altogether. His clients are also sometimes important people, and notably include a King of Bohemia, the King of Scandinavia and a British Prime Minister. He helped the Vatican more than once and was also awarded the Legion of Honour for a case that involved the French Government.

Holmes's character also involves a wish to show off his unique deductive skills and he often prepares elaborate ways to expose or detain an offender in order to impress either Watson or one of the Scotland Yard inspectors.

All in all, and apart from his friendship with Watson (which he values higher than no other) Holmes is a self-confessed loner; he does not wish or attempt to make friends. When telling Watson about his time at college in *The Adventure of the Gloria Scott* he says, "I was never a very sociable fellow, Watson, always rather fond of moping in my rooms and working out my own little methods of thought, so that I never mixed much with the men of my year ... my line of study was quite distinct from that of the other fellows, so that we had no points of contact at all".

With regard to money and finances Holmes's specific costs for his detective services are only occasionally explicitly documented. For example, in *A Scandal in Bohemia*, he is paid an astonishing amount of one thousand pounds (700 in notes and 300 in gold), which was only an advance payment for expenses already accrued on the case. Although Holmes at first needed to share his comfortable residence in Baker Street with Watson to halve the rent costs, it is often suggested that he earns a very good income from his work as a detective. This is evident in *The Final Problem* when, having been paid for his services to the royal house of Scandinavia and the French government, Holmes makes it clear that the money paid was enough for him to retire comfortably.

Morally, Holmes was as virtuous as he could be. Whilst he would not be interested in helping the high, mighty and wealthy unless their case really interested him, he would however help more humble clients for weeks on end if the case really inspired him, regardless of monetary reward.

With regards to women, Conan Doyle remarked to his creative influencer Joseph Bell that "Holmes is as inhuman as a Babbage's calculating machine and just about as likely to fall in love". Although Holmes's life and adventures involve women, notably for example Irene Adler, a retired American opera singer and actress who appears in *A Scandal in Bohemia*, he is really only interested in them if they are involved with a case in some way rather than in a loving relationship sense. Irene Adler was perhaps the only excep-

tion, although Holmes didn't actually fall in love with her, but just held her in high regard. More typically the women in Holmes's life were a means to an end. In *The Adventure of Charles Augustus Milverton*, Holmes gets engaged, but only as a means to an end to extract information that would help him with his case.

In *The Sign of Four*, Watson quotes Holmes as saying, "It is of the first im-

BELOW Sherlock Holmes in *The Adventure of Charles Augustus Milverton*

THE CHARACTER OF SHERLOCK HOLMES

portance not to allow your judgment to be biased by personal qualities. A client is to me a mere unit - a factor in a problem. The emotional qualities are antagonistic to clear reasoning. I assure you that the most winning woman I ever knew was hanged for poisoning three little children for their insurance-money". Regardless of the fact that Holmes wasn't interested in women in any romantic way, Watson makes interesting observations that, despite the fact that Holmes may have an "aversion to women", but nonetheless he has "a peculiarly ingratiating way with [them]."

Apart from the first attempt when Conan Doyle wanted to rid himself of his Sherlock Holmes character, from when he was brought back to the literary world his creator never ended Holmes's life as such, but rather had Holmes retire, which he did in *His Last Bow* when he moved to a small farm on the Sussex Downs. Although the precise date of his retirement is not stated, it is presumed to be before 1904. Holmes takes up beekeeping as a hobby in retirement and he even produces a publication called *Practical Handbook of Bee Culture, with some Observations upon the Segregation of the Queen.* One of the stories that was narrated by Holmes and didn't include Watson at all was *The Adventure of the Lion's Mane.* Published in 1926 but set in 1907, this is one of the last stories in which Holmes is involved in an adventure that took place during his retirement years.

In many ways Sherlock Holmes is a superhero. He seems to always know everything he needs, wins every fight and more. This character would be flat and long forgotten but for the fact that he is a very flawed character. This is a man who uses drugs when he is bored, tends to become depressed, is rude, dismissive of the police and is even a bit lazy. All of these are vital to the character of Sherlock Holmes because without those characteristics, the literature would have been regarded as simple pulp rather than great literature; the Holmes 'canon' would certainly not have stood the test of time in the way that is has if this was the case.

" *It is of the first importance not to allow your judgment to be biased by personal qualities* "

Chapter 3

Sherlock Holmes as a Detective

The first stories of Sherlock Holmes went some way to paint his background and explain how and why Holmes became a superior crime detective and solver.

In *A Study of Scarlet*, and as a chemistry student, he is delighted with the fact that he manages to invent a new method for detecting bloodstains for example. Other early stories also describe how he ends up in a room filled with foul-smelling clouds of fumes after he has indulged in recreational home-chemistry experiments. As to what actually influenced Holmes to become a detective is presented in *The Adventure of the Gloria Scott*. Here it becomes evident that Holmes was greatly influenced by a college friend's father who was highly complimentary about his powers and skills of deduction. Throughout his career as a detective, Holmes only ever focuses on logic and the powers of observation and deduction. His strict adherence to scientific methods is also relentless.

Initially, Holmes is only interested in learning things that are useful to him and he believes that any useless information will just reduce his ability to learn, believing that his mind has a finite capacity to store information. When Watson asked Holmes if he knew that the earth revolved around the sun, Holmes told Watson that the fact was of no real use to him and he would therefore forget it immediately. In *A Study of*

Scarlet, Watson subsequently assesses Holmes's abilities as thus:

1. Knowledge of Literature – nil.
2. Knowledge of Philosophy – nil.
3. Knowledge of Astronomy – nil.
4. Knowledge of Politics – Feeble.
5. Knowledge of Botany – Variable. Well up in belladonna, opium and poisons generally. Knows nothing of practical gardening.
6. Knowledge of Geology – Practical, but limited. Tells at a glance different soils from each other. After walks, has shown me splashes upon his trousers, and told me by their colour and consistence in what part of London he had received them.
7. Knowledge of Chemistry – Profound.
8. Knowledge of Anatomy – Accurate, but unsystematic.
9. Knowledge of Sensational Literature – Immense. He appears to know every detail of every horror perpetrated in the century.
10. Plays the violin well.
11. Is an expert singlestick player, boxer and swordsman.
12. Has a good practical knowledge of British law.

ABOVE Illustration of the short story *A Scandal in Bohemia*, which appeared in The Strand Magazine in July, 1891

Of course, as Holmes's character develops through later stories, some aspects of the above list become contradictory. His supposed ignorance with regard to politics for example is superseded in *A Scandal in Bohemia* when Holmes instantly recognises the real identity of the supposed 'Count von Kramm'. In fact, Holmes's knowledge and understanding of several of the above subjects that Watson originally commented on showed much improvement in later stories. With regard to literature, Holmes would refer to the Bible, Shakespeare and even Goethe. His feelings towards Watson's opinion of

SHERLOCK HOLMES AS A DETECTIVE

him in this regard is sarcastically highlighted in *The Hound of the Baskervilles* when he recognises works by influential eighteenth-century English painter Sir Joshua Reynolds and Austrian-Italian painter Martin Knoller. Holmes rebukes Watson by saying, "Excuse the admiration of a connoisseur ... Watson won't allow that I know anything of art, but that is mere jealousy, since our views upon the subject differ.

The notion that Holmes disregards or isn't interested in any knowledge

that isn't useful or immediately relevant to him as a detective also changes and is abandoned in the later stories. In fact in *The Valley of Fear*, Holmes actually states that "all knowledge comes useful to the detective" and also in *The Adventure of the Lion's Mane* he describes himself as "an omnivorous reader with a strangely retentive memory for trifles".

With regard to Holmes's actual methods of detection, he employs many, but they all stem from that of 'abductive' reasoning. This is a form of logical inference that goes from observation to a hypothesis that accounts for the reliable data (observation) and seeks to explain relevant evidence. The American philosopher Charles Sanders Peirce (1839–1914) first introduced the term as 'guessing'. Peirce said that to 'abduce' a hypothetical explanation from an observed surprising circumstance is to surmise that may be true because then would be a matter of course. Thus, to abduce from involves determining that is sufficient (or nearly sufficient), but not necessary. One statement that Holmes quite often said is, "When you have eliminated the impossible, whatever remains, however improbable, must be the truth".

Holmes also employs the process of deductive reasoning. This is the process of reasoning from one or more general statements or premises to reach a logically certain conclusion. Deductive reasoning links premises with conclusions. If all premises are true, the terms are clear, and the rules of deductive logic are followed, then the conclusion reached

SHERLOCK HOLMES AS A DETECTIVE

is necessarily true. In *A Scandal in Bohemia*, a good example of this is seen when Holmes deduces Watson's situation just by looking at his shoes. When an astonished Watson asks Holmes how he knows this, Holmes explains, 'It is simplicity itself ... My eyes tell me that on the inside of your left shoe, just where the firelight strikes it, the leather is scored by six almost parallel cuts. Obviously they have been caused by someone who has very carelessly scraped round the edges of the sole in order to remove crusted mud from it. Hence, you see, my double deduction that you had been out in vile weather, and that you had a particularly malignant boot-slitting specimen of the London slavery.'

Amongst other things, Holmes is also a competent cryptanalyst. This is the study of analysing information systems in order to study the hidden aspects of the systems. An example of this can be found in *The Adventure of the Dancing Men*, when Holmes uses frequency analysis to solve a puzzle. As he says to Watson, "I am fairly familiar with all forms of secret writing, and am myself the author of a trifling monograph upon the subject, in which I analyse one hundred and sixty separate ciphers".

Of course Holmes also analyses lots of physical evidence, and all in a precise and scientific way. Not only does he use cigarette butts, tobacco ash, the use of gunpowder residue and an early use of fingerprint analysis to identify offenders, but the classic analysis of latent prints, such as bicycle tracks, hoof prints and footprints all play their part in his crime solving adventures.

With regard to personal protection, both Holmes and Watson carry pistols with them and Watson writes about the weapons being used on seven separate occasions. For example, in *The Hound of the Baskervilles*, both of them shoot at the hound; in *The Adventure of the Empty House*, Colonel Sebastian Moran is pistol-whipped by Watson; and in *The Musgrave Ritual*, Holmes creates a patriotic V.R. (Victoria Regina) in the wall of

SHERLOCK HOLMES AS A DETECTIVE

his Baker Street residence with bullets.

In addition to having firearms to hand, Holmes is also pretty handy when it comes to hand-to-hand combat. Examples of this can be seen in numerous combat situations Holmes finds himself in throughout the stories and naturally, he inevitably emerges from these confrontations as the victorious one. In *The Sign of Four*, Holmes introduces himself to a prizefighter as, "The amateur who fought three rounds with you at Alison's rooms on the night of your benefit four years back." McMurdo responds by saying, "Ah, you're one that has wasted your gifts, you have! You might have aimed high, if you had joined the fancy." In *Gloria Scott* and *The Yellow Face* references to Holmes being a trained boxer is also apparent: Watson said of Holmes that, "he was undoubtedly one of the finest boxers of his weight that I have ever seen".

As well as bare-knuckle fighting, Holmes also demonstrates skills in other areas of combat, including the martial arts. In particular, when recounting the story to Watson about how he used martial arts to overcome his enemy Professor Moriarty, managing to throw his adversary to his death at the famous

Reichenbach Falls in Switzerland, Holmes states, "I have some knowledge, however, of *baritsu*, or the Japanese system of wrestling, which has more than once been very useful to me". Baritsu is a real yet eclectic martial art that was originally developed in England during the years 1898 to 1902. It was essentially a combination of Jujutsu (a Japanese martial art and a method of close combat for defeating an armed and armored opponent in which one uses no weapon or only a short weapon) with boxing and cane fencing.

SHERLOCK HOLMES AS A DETECTIVE

Holmes's strong physical strength is also made apparent, which is arguably essential bearing in mind that he usually won any combat situation he found himself in. In several stories, Holmes is described as having fantastic physical strength and most certainly above average. In addition to straightening out a steel poker with his bare hands in *The Adventure of the Speckled Band*, in *The Yellow Face*, Watson makes the observation about Holmes that "Few men were capable of greater muscular effort".

Other methods of defence are either alluded to or in fact used throughout the Sherlock Holmes stories, including the cane that he carries, which is actually used twice as a weapon and Watson describes Holmes as being an expert at singlestick. Although none of the stories depicts Holmes actually using a sword, in *A Study of Scarlet*, Watson describes Holmes as an expert in using one if necessary. One of Holmes's favourite weapons, as described in *The Six Napoleons*, is the riding or hunting crop. In *A Case of Identity* he nearly thrashed a swindler with it and in *The Red-Headed League*, he knocks a pistol out of an adversary's hand.

And were would a world-famous detective like Sherlock Holmes be without the necessary skills of disguise and in conjunction with that, acting. Well, Holmes displays a very strong aptitude for both and throughout Doyle's stories Holmes often uses disguise whilst working undercover to gather evidence in order to solve a case. His acting skills are also invaluable when he needs to feign illness or being wounded. This would happen particularly if it would affect his case in a positive way or help to successfully incriminate those he wanted to be incriminated. Watson himself often fell for Holmes's disguises and in *A Scandal of Bohemia* he remarks that "The stage lost a fine actor ..., when [Holmes] became a specialist in crime".

Chapter 4

The Influence of Sherlock Holmes

The influence that Sherlock Holmes has had on many aspects of life since he became part of the literary world is quite prolific. In terms of academic study, many have become scholars of Holmes and Watson and study their world as if they were actually real people. Some have dedicated years to studying and dissecting Conan Doyle's literature in order to gain an in-depth knowledge and understanding of every aspect of Holmes and Watson's life, adventures and methods of detection.

With regard to literature specifically, there were other fictional detectives before and after Sherlock Holmes. Edgar Allan Poe's C. Auguste Dupin and Emile Gaboriau's Monsieur Lecoq both influenced Conan Doyle. After Holmes, and due to the popularity of the genre at the time, many authors went on to create fictional investigative detectives: Agatha Christie with Hercule Poirot and Dorothy L. Sayers' Lord Peter Wimsey for example. However, Conan Doyle created a character that, although not the first ever fictional detective, has become a worldwide phenomenon nonetheless and Holmes is arguably the most famous and iconic fictional detective in the world.

In view of the fact that the Royal Society of Chemistry bequeathed an honorary fellowship to Sherlock Holmes says a lot about how, even though fictional, his impact and influence with regard to his use of forensic science and analytical

" Holmes often concentrated on finding trace evidence such as tobacco ash, hair and fingerprints "

chemistry has had in both popular literature and the real world of forensic science.

At the time that Conan Doyle was writing the Sherlock Holmes stories, many of the techniques and methods used by Holmes were very much in their infancy; he was therefore a leading, pioneering and inspirational character with regard to forensic science in literature and many of the techniques he used, developed and became widely accepted and mainstream.

Holmes insisted on studying a crime scene in detail with his magnifying glass to hand and constantly complained about a crime scene being contaminated before it was analysed properly, continually emphasising the critical importance of its integrity being left in tact so that proper examinations could be carried out. This is something that is now paramount to any crime scene examination, which is why the police and forensic experts now immediately cordon off areas to be investigated in order to avoid any contamination of existing evidence.

Holmes famously made great use of trace evidence. Trace evidence is created when objects come into contact with each other leaving traces that can be identified and analysed. Trace evidence became an important part of criminal investigations during the early twentieth century and was used to solve homicides as well as being intrinsic to accident investigation, where typically movement or contact of two parts would leave a telltale mark that can then be investigated. Examples of typical trace evidence in criminal cases include fingerprints, glove prints, hairs, footprints, botanical material etc.

Holmes often concentrated on finding trace evidence such as tobacco ash, hair and fingerprints, and although he frequently used his magnifying glass at the crime scene, he also had an optical microscope at his home in Baker Street to investigate traces further. In fact, Holmes seems to have had a small home chemistry laboratory set up because he not only analysed trace evidence, but also carried out examinations of blood residue as well as employing toxicology experiments in order to determine whether a poison had been involved in the crime in question. This was evident in *The Adventure of the Naval Treaty* for example.

In addition to these laboratory and investigative skills, Holmes was also a dab hand when it came to analysing handwriting, known as questioned document examination or QDE. Still a forensic science discipline today, QDE is used to provide evidence about a suspicious or questionable document that requires a variety of scientific methods and processes in order to ascertain any proof. Typically QDE will be used to prove or disprove aspects such as damage to a document, forgery, authenticity, origin and where the document has been, as well as who has had possession of it. The examination of handwriting is the most common method of investigation and this is something that Holmes also excelled at when testing police or his own theories about a situation.

Holmes's forensic science abilities were really very advanced for the time and he even employed ballistics (the

science of mechanics that deals with the launching, flight and behaviour and effects of projectiles) to help him solve a case. In *The Adventure of the Empty House*, for example, Holmes collected spent bullets from the crime scene and then measured and matched their calibre (the approximate internal diameter of the bullet) with a suspected murder weapon.

Last but by no means least, Holmes's intellect, basic instinct, perception and deductive skills also played a huge part when it came to solving his cases. He would assess every bit of his clients and suspects with regard to how they dressed, noting things like the state of their clothes, plus anything noteworthy such as clay on someone's boots. He would also take their physical condition and their general state of mind into account, as well as homing in on physical attributes such as skin blemishes or tattoos for example, which could reveal important clues as to a person's past history. Holmes also employed the same techniques with actual personal items that a person may have about their body. He employed these techniques famously in *The Hound of the Baskervilles* with regard to walking sticks, as well as hats in the case of *The Blue Carbuncle.*

Chapter 5

The Legacy of Sherlock Holmes

RIGHT Written by American actor and playwright William Gillette in conjunction with Conan Doyle, Sherlock Holmes, a play in four acts was first performed in New York City on 6th November 1899

Holmes's character has been translated to other a plethora of other forms of media, and he is widely known on both stage and screen. The earliest actor to have essayed the role is William Gillette (a founding member of the New York Holmes Society still known as the Baker Street Irregulars), who gave several popular theatrical portrayals at the turn of the 20th century. Those who have appeared as Holmes on-screen include Basil Rathbone, Peter Cushing, Jeremy Brett, Robert Downey Jr., and Benedict Cumberbatch.

Ironically, two of the iconic emblems associated with Holmes - his meerschaum pipe and deerstalker hat - are not actually original to Conan Doyle's writings. Gillette introduced the curved meerschaum pipe (it is thought to have been easier on the actor's jaw during a long performance), and Sidney Paget the deerstalker (or 'fore-and-aft') cap - it was, after all, de rigueur for country living - in more than one illustration for *The Strand* of Holmes at work on his investigations in the country.

In addition to a myriad of translations of the Holmes adventures throughout the world, a genre of parodies and pastiches has also developed based upon the Sherlock Holmes character. An entire collection of more scholarly 'higher criticism' of Conan Doyle's writings also exists that was initiated by Ronald Knox's *Studies in the Literature of Sherlock Holmes*, which was published in 1912.

THE LEGACY OF SHERLOCK HOLMES

More recent higher criticism is epitomised by the work appearing in *The Baker Street Journal* (founded in 1946), a quarterly publication of the Baker Street Irregulars. Holmes devotees, known as Sherlockians or Holmesians, frequently gather in societies around the world to pay tribute to the master detective with cultist fervour. The most established of these societies are the Baker Street Irregulars, founded in 1934, and the Sherlock Holmes Society of London, founded in 1951. The latter traces its origins to the Sherlock Holmes Society that was formed in London in 1934 and counted among its members the scholar and writer Dorothy L. Sayers; it had ceased its activities by the 1940s however.

Having read thus far it should perhaps be of no surprise to learn that the Guinness World Records lists Sherlock Holmes frequently as the 'most portrayed movie character'. Sherlock Holmes has been the star in more than two hundred films with over seventy actors having the privilege of portraying the famous detective. The very first portrayal of Holmes on the screen, albeit in a now barely recognisable form, was produced in 1900 and was called *Sherlock Holmes Baffled*. Directed by cinematographer Arthur Marvin, this was a very short (thirty seconds in fact) silent film made in America, which was intended to be shown on the Mutoscope, an early motion picture device.

ADAPTATIONS

Not only was Conan Doyle's Sherlock Holmes literature immensely popular, but Holmes became the subject of much popular interest with regard to adaptations, initially for the stage, radio, then for film and later still for the television. This is also not to mention comic strips, comic books, music and, from the mid-1980s with the computer age beginning to take full flight, Sherlock Holmes video games. A list compiled by Ronald B. DeWaal in 1995 at the time listed over twenty-five thousand Sherlock Holmes-related productions and products; quite staggering bearing in mind that was nearly twenty years ago.

It would be impossible to therefore cover every Sherlock Holmes adaptation ever made here, this would arguably be a book in its own right, but there are some notable adaptations that should be highlighted to show just how much impact Holmes had and still has.

Written by American actor and playwright William Gillette in conjunction with Conan Doyle, *Sherlock Holmes*, a play in four acts was first performed in New York City on 6th November 1899. Whilst there was much new material, the play drew its material from three of Doyle's already published stories: *A Scandal in Bohemia*, *The Final Problem*, and *A Study in Scarlet*

THE LEGACY OF SHERLOCK HOLMES

and it ran for more than two hundred and sixty performances. The play then toured the United States before moving to the Lyceum Theatre in London, where it was premiered in September 1901. The play was also well received in London and it ran for two hundred performances. Gillette also revived the play in 1905, 1910 and 1915.

Even though Gillette actually wrote the play, because the plot and some of the dialogue was directly lifted from Doyle's original stories, Doyle was credited as being the co-author. Gillette, much to the unease of Doyle at first, took some liberties with the Holmes character, giving him a love interest for example that was modelled on the role of the female character Irene Adler in *A Scandal in Bohemia*. Gillette renamed her Alice Faulkner. Due to the success of the play Doyle's reluctance to let Gillette do whatever he wanted with his beloved detective relented somewhat and he said, "I was charmed both with the play, the acting, and the pecuniary result".

Interestingly, Gillette's play also had a reverse influence on Doyle and his later writings. Although the character of an unnamed pageboy existed in *A Case of Identity*, it was Gillette who used the

character in his play and gave him the name 'Billy'. Doyle later himself reintroduced the same character into some Holmes stories and he adopted the name Billy too. Professor Moriarty was also the villain in Gillette's play, but until the play he had never been referred to as anything other than that. It was Gillette who christened him 'Robert Moriarty' in fact. The working relationship that grew between Doyle and Gillette can be seen when Doyle recounted how he reacted to a cable he received from Gillette asking him if he was allowed to marry Holmes off. Doyle's response was, "You may marry him, murder him, or do anything you like to him".

Initially, Gillette himself played Sherlock Holmes, but the role was later taken over by English actor and playwright Harry Arthur Saintsbury. In addition to being an early mentor of Charlie Chaplin (who in fact played Billy the pageboy in the play at the age of thirteen), Saintsbury became known for his portrayal of the famous detective and played the part more than a thousand times in total by 1916.

Since its first performance in 1899, the *Sherlock Holmes* play has been adapted many times during the twentieth century. Described as 'the most elaborate of the early movies', a silent film of the play was produced in 1916, which featured Gillette as Holmes. The play was again filmed in 1922 with John Barrymore as Holmes and again in 1932 when Clive Brook took the leading role. Back on the stage, the play was also revived by The Royal Shakespeare Company in 1973. It was directed by Frank Dunlop and starred John Wood as Holmes. The production was such a great success that it went on to be produced on Broadway and then went on tour.

Gillette's portrayal of Holmes went a long way in creating the modern image of the detective and he used the deerstalker cap and the curved pipe in the 1916 motion picture, which of course became durable and iconic symbols of the character. This was emphasised following the Holmes illustrations that were drawn by British illustrator Sidney Paget and published in *The Strand* magazine.

Following the success of the Gillette collaboration, Doyle wrote and produced a play based on *The Adventure of the Speckled Band*, which premiered at the Adelphi Theatre in London on 4th June 1910; Holmes was played by Saintsbury.

Between 1921 and 1923 a series of silent black-and-white films were produced by Stoll Pictures. Starring British actor Eille Norwood as Holmes and Hubert Willis as Dr. Watson, forty-five short and two feature films were made. The two actors co-starred with each other for all, except the final film, *The Sign of Four*, in which Willis was replaced by actor Arthur Cullin.

Although the 1929 film *The Return of Sherlock Holmes* was made in a silent version for those picture houses that couldn't accommodate sound, this was in fact the first Sherlock Holmes film to have sound. It was filmed in New York City, written by Basil Dean with Clive Brook starring as Sherlock Holmes.

With sounds and pictures fully developed, fourteen Sherlock Holmes films were made in the United States between 1939 and 1946, and all of them starred Basil Rathbone as Sherlock Holmes and Nigel Bruce as Dr. Watson. Two of the films were made for 20th Century Fox and the other twelve for Universal Pictures. The latter of the production companies made their mark on the look and feel of the films by giving them a contemporary setting, which was obviously then the post-World War II era. The 20th Century Fox version of *The Hound of the Baskervilles*, produced in 1939,

is also famous for using the somewhat controversial reference to Holmes's drug-taking habits; the final line of the film being, "Watson, the needle".

1959 was the year that saw the first Sherlock Holmes screen appearance in colour with Hammer Film Productions' *The Hound of the Baskervilles*, starring English actor Peter Cushing. Not only did Cushing become a regular actor for many Hammer films, but he also played Sherlock Holmes many times over the years in both film and television productions.

From these early stage and film productions of Sherlock Holmes adaptations sprang a plethora of non-canonical Sherlock Holmes works. From 1898, right up to the present day derivative works, whether it is films, television series or books, all have been produced and still continue to be so. The life of Sherlock Holmes and Dr. Watson has and still has a profound influence on others.

Again, there are far too many to document each one here, but it is possible to give an idea of the sort of derivative works and diversity of them that have been produced throughout the latter half of the twentieth century.

In terms of literature, the characteristics of the original Holmes, as both an excellent logician and a phenomenal fighter, has been highly influential with regard to inspiring other authors to create characters with similar skills. Some use his name and others create their own central character but rework typical Holmes exploits and plots into their own work.

First published in 1954, *The Exploits of Sherlock Holmes*, is a short story collection of twelve Sherlock Holmes pastiches that was written by Adrian Conan Doyle and John Dickson Carr. Adrian was the youngest son of Sir Arthur Conan Doyle and John Dickson Carr was Sir Arthur Conan Doyle's official biographer. The stories in the collection are as follows:

> *The Adventure of the Seven Clocks*
> *The Adventure of the Gold Hunter*
> *The Adventure of the Wax Gamblers*
> *The Adventure of the Highgate Miracle*
> *The Adventure of the Black Baronet*
> *The Adventure of the Sealed Room*
> *The Adventure of the Foulkes Rath*
> *The Adventure of the Abbas Ruby*
> *The Adventure of the Dark Angels*
> *The Adventure of the Two Women*
> *The Adventure of the Deptford Horror*
> *The Adventure of the Red Widow*

Whilst there is some debate with regard to who was the author of what and sometimes the parallels with the canonical stories are too close for comfort, *The Exploits of Sherlock Holmes*, is viewed as one of the earliest and most authoritative examples of Sherlockian pastiche. Not surprisingly therefore, the works hold great interest with Holmesian collectors. In 1963, however, John Murray divided the stories into two: *The Exploits of Sherlock Holmes* by Adrian Conan Doyle, which contained the last six stories listed above and *More Exploits of Sherlock Holmes* by Adrian Conan Doyle and John Dickson Carr, which contained the first six stories.

Written by American author Nicholas Meyer, *The Seven-Per-Cent Solution: Being a Reprint from the Reminiscences of John H. Watson, M.D.*, is another good example of a derivative Holmes pastiche. The novel, which was published in 1974 as a 'lost manuscript' of the late Dr. John H. Watson, is a pastiche of a Sherlock Holmes adventure. The story recounts Holmes's recovery from cocaine addiction and his subsequent efforts to prevent war within Europe, which is unraveled through a sinister kidnapping plot. The novel met with

much critical acclaim and made *The New York Times* Best Seller list for forty weeks between September 1974 and June 1975. In the *Publishers Weekly* list of bestselling novels from 1974 the work was ranked at number nine. It was then made into a film, with the same name, in 1976. Meyer then went on to write two further Sherlock Holmes pastiches: *The West End Horror*, which was published in 1976 and *The Canary Trainer*, published in 1993.

Just before the turn of the century a science fiction version, *Sherlock Holmes in the 22nd Century*, was first broadcast in 1999. This was an animated television series in which Sherlock Holmes was brought back to life in the twenty-second century. Created by Sandy Ross and written by Eleanor Burian-Mohr, the series ran for two seasons, totaling twenty-six episodes and it was nominated for a Daytime Emmy for Special Class Animated Programme.

Starring Michael Caine and Ben Kingsley, 1988 saw a British comedy film released called *Without a Clue*, the description on the cover sleeve being 'Two of the world's greatest actors having the time of their lives in the most hilarious Sherlock Holmes adventure of them all'. Directed by Thom Eberhardt, the plot is based on the fact that Dr. Watson (Ben Kingsley) creates a fictional character, which is Holmes, to enable him to solve crimes incognito. Watson ends up hiring an unemployed actor, Reginald Kincaid (Michael Caine) to play the part of the fictional detective in order to satisfy public demand to see Holmes in person.

Without a Clue is one of several Sherlock Holmes spoofs and this one had two particularly notable aspects: the main characters were reversed, culminating in a bumbling Holmes with Watson being the genius detective; and in the film, Watson gets tired of his fictional creation of Holmes and tries to get him out of his life, but he is forced to bring him back by popular demand. This is the mirror image of the real situation when Conan Doyle tried unsuccessfully to kill Holmes off and had to bring him back, also due to popular demand.

The film received mixed views from the critics, but it is frequently included in the 'top 10' lists of Sherlock films. American film critic Roger Ebert wasn't so convinced and comments, '*Without a Clue* begins with the premise that Sherlock Holmes never existed; that the man known as 'Holmes' was, in fact, a third-rate actor named Reginald Kincaid, and he was hired by Dr. John Watson to play the role. This is an amusing premise, but it is not enough.'

Finally, and to highlight just how global the Sherlock Holmes phenomenon had become by the end of the twentieth century, an anime television series, based on Conan Doyle's canonic Sherlock Holmes stories, called *Sherlock Hound* was created and produced in Japan. Consisting of twenty-six episodes, *Sherlock Hound* was broadcast between 1984 and 1985 and almost all of the characters were anthropomorphic dogs. The anime series contained all of the main Holmes characters in the form of dogs, including Sherlock Hound, Doctor Watson, Mrs. Hudson, Professor Moriarty and Inspector Lestrade.

THE GREAT GAME

The Great Game is the popular hobby of trying to resolve anomalies as well as attempting to shed light on details about Sherlock Holmes and Dr. Watson that are merely implied from the Conan Doyle Sherlock Holmes canon of fifty-six short stories and four novels. The Great Game is also known as the Holmesian Game, the Sherlockian Game or simply the Game. Those who play the Great Game view and treat both Holmes and Watson as if they are real people. The idea being that by combining knowledge and research about the historical era when the actual stories were written with detailed aspects of the canonical stories, accurate yet imaginative biographies can be compiled about both characters, and people (as those who play the game would say). The English author Mollie Hardwick, who wrote many books and plays based around the Sherlock Holmes novels, once described the Sherlockian Game as a huge family joke.

The Great Game began in the early twentieth century when the first Holmesian scholars started studying Doyle's Sherlock Holmes canon of fiction as if the characters were in fact non-fiction. Sherlockian essays were published by Frank Sidgwick and Arthur Bartlett Maurice in 1902, but initially they didn't receive much recognition or attention. More notable early Holmesian scholars included English priest, theologian, writer and regular broadcaster Ronald Knox and American journalist, novelist, essayist and poet Christopher Morley.

Creator of the detective Lord Peter Wimsey, Dorothy L. Sayers also wrote several speculative Holmesian essays, which were later published in her 1951 *Unpopular Opinions*. In the foreword of the book she notes that, 'The game of applying the methods of the 'Higher Criticism' to the Sherlock Holmes canon was begun, many years ago, by Monsignor Ronald Knox, with the aim of showing that, by those methods, one could disintegrate a modern classic as speciously as a certain school of critics have endeavoured to disintegrate the Bible. Since then, the thing has become a hobby among a select set of jesters here and in America'. A further comment that Sayers made about the Great Game was that it 'must be played as solemnly as a county cricket match at Lord's; the slightest touch of extravagance or burlesque ruins the atmosphere'.

In fact, the essay that Ronald Knox wrote and issued when he was a student at Oxford University titled *Studies in the Literature of Sherlock Holmes*, is now regarded as one of the founding texts of Holmesian scholarship. Knox's essay was re-printed along with others in 1928 and this sparked a series of reactions. A year later, Sydney Roberts, a professor at Cam-

bridge University responded to Knox's arguments in a booklet entitled *A Note on the Watson Problem*. Following this S. C. Roberts then produced a complete Watson biography and T.S. Blakeney also wrote a Holmesian-based book. Other early Holmesian's of note also include the American bibliographer and book collector Vincent Starrett and the archaeologist Harold Wilmerding Bell. All of this Holmes scholarly activity hence culminated in the birth of the Great Game.

The Great Game in its traditional form concentrates on the study and therefore explanation of contradictions that occur throughout the Holmes canon. For example, in *A Study in Scarlet*, Watson has a war wound that is described as being in his shoulder, yet in *The Sign of Four*, it has moved to his leg. His first name is John in the aforementioned book and *The Problem of Thor Bridge*, but changes to James in *The Man with the Twisted Lip*.

Other popular areas that the Great Game focuses on include Holmes's actual birthdate; which university he went to – Oxford, Cambridge or both; and Holmes's mental health and emotional state, which has been a topic of debate and analysis within the Game for decades.

The original literature of Conan Doyle was used by Dorothy Sayers and many of the early Holmesians as the chief basis for their speculations, but a more fanciful school of playing the Great Game started to emerge during the middle of the twentieth century.

The more modern and shifted game was first represented by William S. Baring-Gould, who is best known as the author of the influential 1962 fictional biography, *Sherlock Holmes of Baker Street: A life of the world's first consulting detective.*

Several personal 'biographies' of Holmes followed, one of the more recent ones being the 2006 *Sherlock Holmes: The Unauthorized Biography*, written by Nick Rennison. In fact, this is a non-canonical Sherlock Holmes pastiche novel. In an interview, the author says about his book, 'So, really, the book is three strands woven together. There's the material from the Conan Doyle stories, there's the real history of the 19th century, and if those two failed to provide something, then I was in a position where I could simply make it up.'

Perhaps the most prolific and recent of Holmesian scholarly work has been recently completed having started in 1998. American attorney and writer Leslie S. Klinger edited and annotated *The Sherlock Holmes Reference Library: Complete set of ten volumes.* To be published by Gasogene Books (a publisher dedicated to the study of Sherlock Holmes and his world, and an imprint of Wessex Press) in 2014, the culmination of work consists of (as described by the publisher themselves):

The original, exhaustively annotated, ten-volume edition of the Sherlock Holmes stories by Edgar Award winner Leslie S. Klinger. It's the most complete collection of Sherlockian scholarship and commentary ever assembled. No Sherlockian bookshelf is complete without this landmark series. As is well known, the adventures of Sherlock Holmes have inspired a vast body of literature dedicated to the proposition that the Great Detective was not a mere work of fiction, *but an actual historical person.* Since the 1920s these 'writings about The Writings' have contributed fascinating new insights into the stories, enhancing the pleasure of reading them. *The Sherlock Holmes Reference Library* puts the entire history of this 'Higher Criticism' at your fingertips! Each illustrated volume is bursting with scholarly annotations and features a

THE LEGACY OF SHERLOCK HOLMES

sturdy, smythe-sewn soft cover binding.

The finished ten-volume reference library has already met with great literary and scholarly praise indeed:

> *"The Sherlock Holmes Reference Library is a publishing triumph!"*
> (Michael Cox, Executive Producer, Granada Television's *Sherlock Holmes*)

> *"The standards of scholarship and production [of the series]...have never faltered. A wonderful project, excellently carried out. Highest recommendation."*
> (Roger Johnson, The Sherlock Holmes Society of London)

> *"If you want to master just about everything there is to know about The Great Detective and The Good Doctor, to understand what Holmes meant when he referred to "a comet vintage" of wine, and to know what discrepancies there are between the English and American editions of the works, plus a thousand other things relating to Holmes, Watson, and the England of the Victorian era, you must have these volumes."*
> (Otto Penzler, The Mysterious Bookshop)

SOCIETIES

There are now many Sherlock Holmes Societies all over the world, including in Australia, India and Japan, some of which have been operating for many years. In New York, the Baker Street Irregulars was founded in 1934 and the society is still active to this day. In the same year, the Sherlock Holmes Society in London was also founded, but the society was dissolved in 1937. This London-based society was, however, relaunched in 1951 and it is still going strong today. The original 1934 society in New York also triggered many more offshoots of Holmesian circles and these were known as 'scion societies'.

The concept for the relaunch of the Sherlock Holmes Society of London was initiated in 1950 when St. Marylebone Borough Council were trying to decide what to do to celebrate the Festival of Britain, which was to take place the following year. It was in fact the Public Libraries Committee who suggested an exhibition about Sherlock Holmes. The idea was not, however, welcomed by all on the council committee, who viewed the idea as absurd and questioned the idea as absurd and questioned whether focusing on a fictional character who was associated with murky crime was really the best idea and suggestion they could come up with.

In the end, however, public opinion put pressure on the council to go ahead with the concept. Following seventeen letters that were published in *The Times*, the council eventually agreed and the planning of the exhibition got underway, being led by a small group of Sherlock Holmes enthusiasts.

The result of all the petitioning and planning was an absolute triumph in the end, with over 54,000 people visiting the Sherlock Holmes exhibition during the Festival of Britain. In addition to the Sherlock Holmes enthusiasts who had written letters to *The Times* offering support and mementoes, the exhibition actually meticulously recreated the famous sitting room at 221B Baker Street. The exhibits included a Persian slipper for Holmes's tobacco, a gasogene for Watson's soda, a jack-knife for Holmes to skewer his unanswered correspondence to the mantelpiece with, not to mention the attention to detail in the form of fresh crumpets – supplied every day by the local bakery – and in which two different sets of teeth were in.

Following the total success of the exhibition, the question was naturally asked, why doesn't the original Sherlock Holmes Society of London reform. Originally, the 1930s society was very small, yet it did have a very distinguished following of scholars, including the leading cleric H. R. L. 'Dick' Sheppard, formerly of St. Martin in the Fields, and the crime writer Dorothy L. Sayers.

So, in 1951 the new Sherlock Holmes Society of London was founded. The following May saw the publication of the first Sherlock Holmes Journal that included articles about Holmes's personality and Dr. Watson's gambling habits, plus a review of the film of *The Hound of the Baskervilles*. At the time the membership numbers were just over one hundred and thirty.

It didn't take long for the society to adopt a schedule and pattern activities, which it still follows today. The society had regular meetings, published a twice-yearly journal and always held an annual dinner every January. Although the tone of the society was always scholarly, it was also both witty and not too heavy. The society has been described as family like, whose skills and responsibilities are passed down from one generation to the next.

A particular aspect that the society triumphed in was the celebrated pilgrimage to Switzerland in 1968. At least forty members of the society were accompanied by just as many members of the Press and all dressed in full Victorian costume. At the Reichenbach Falls, Lord Gore-Booth (President of the Society at the time) shed his cloak as Head of the Diplomatic Service to become Sherlock Holmes himself. The evil Professor Moriarty was also present, in the guise of leading barrister Charles Scholefield and the pair locked themselves in the famous death struggle. The impact of this fight changed the reputation of the Society forever when the BBC made it the very first news bulletin item; the Society had reached a new level of exposure and success for the first time.

There have since been five pilgrimages to Switzerland. In 1993, the Society made its first visit to France. Full costume was again *de rigeur* as members visited Bordeaux and Cognac, concluding in Montpellier, where Holmes had spent part of his exile while the entire world believed him to be dead, exactly one hundred years earlier. And in 2001, to celebrate its 50th birthday, the Society took a cruise in the Baltic, with visits to

The Sherlock Holmes Society of
London organise trips to Switzerland

THE LEGACY OF SHERLOCK HOLMES

Oslo, Stockholm, Copenhagen, Tallinn, St Petersburg and Helsinki.

The United Kingdom is not neglected in the Society's peregrinations either. Summer weekend trips have included expeditions to Dartmoor to visit the scene of *The Hound of the Baskervilles*, to the Peak District in the north to explore the territory of *The Priory School*, and to both Oxford and Cambridge. Needless to say, controversy rages in the Society as to which of these two was actually Holmes's university.

The Sherlock Holmes Society of London was and still is a society that is open to anyone who has an interest in Sherlock Holmes, Dr. John H. Watson and their world and the membership numbers exceed one thousand. The society continues the tradition that the small group of enthusiasts initiated more than forty years ago.

Membership of the society today is just as varied and interesting as it ever was and, as described by the society themselves: the Society holds regular meetings, usually in London. Members and guests gather for drinks and chat, followed by dinner for those who wish it, and then a paper or a panel discussion on some aspect of the life and work of Sherlock Holmes. Contributions from the floor are welcomed, and usually develop into a lively debate, which might well be continued in the bar afterwards. The focus for the event might be on a particular case, or on a special subject such as music, transport, food and wine, science, police work, literary influences ... the possibilities are endless. Sometimes the scholarship is replaced by a novelty evening – there have been two or three mock trials, a music hall entertainment, a Mastermind and a University Challenge. There are also less formal events – pub gatherings and London walks are popular, as is the Film Evening. Each year there is either a weekend trip or a day out, visiting scenes of Holmes's cases outside London. The Society has also instigated an annual London Weekend, with events on three or four successive days, making it worthwhile for Members from abroad or from other parts of the UK to come to and stay in the capital.

The interest in Sherlock Holmes is still very much a worldwide phenomenon and the Society, although based in London, still embraces Sherlock Holmes enthusiasts from all walks of life and from every corner of the globe.

The reconstructed Sherlock Holmes sitting room that was created during the 1951 Festival of Britain was the masterpiece of the Sherlock Holmes Exhibition and it included an exclusive collection of original material. Once the exhibition had finished, the exhibited Holmes items were then moved. Some items were sent to the Conan Doyle Collection in Lucens in Switzerland and some were transferred to the Sherlock Holmes Pub in Westminster, London. Both of these exhibitions focused on recreating Holmes and Watson's Baker Street sitting room and both are still open for the public to see.

In 1990, the world saw its very first museum open that was entirely dedicated to a fictional character. It is perhaps not surprising to learn that this was and still is to be found in Baker Street in London. Although the privately-run museum is in fact situated between numbers 237 and 241, the glass above the front door is marked with 221B by permission of the City of Westminster. The museum is run by the Sherlock Holmes Society of England, a non-profit organisation

1891 1991

• AT THIS FEARFUL PLACE, SHERLOCK HOLMES VANQUISHED PROFESSOR MORIARTY, ON 4 MAY 1891.

• AN DIESEM FURCHTERREGENDEN ORT BESIEGTE SHERLOCK HOLMES AM 4. MAI 1891 PROFESSOR MORIARTY.

• A CET ENDROIT TERRIFIANT, SHERLOCK HOLMES A VAINCU LE PROFESSEUR MORIARTY LE 4 MAI, 1891.

Erected by ★ errichtet von ★ erigé par
The Bimetallic Question of Montréal and
The Reichenbach Irregulars of Switzerland

THE LEGACY OF SHERLOCK HOLMES

and being entirely focused on Sherlock
Holmes, the museum only exhibits material relating to the fictional character
and not Conan Doyle. Doyle's second
daughter, Dame Jean Conan Doyle, was
actually never a supporter of the museum
because she didn't agree with reinforcing
the attitude (adhered to by many Holmes
fans and enthusiasts) that Holmes was a
real person who really existed.

Despite the fact that Holmes was
only ever a fictional character, there are
many who prefer to live in the imaginary
world themselves and think of him as a
person who did really exist. Outside the
Baker Street museum is a commemora-
tive blue plaque that states the years
that Holmes supposedly resided there.
Although the plaque is very similar in
design to those that English Heritage
put up, they were not responsible for the
Holmes one because they really do only
erect plaques to commemorate people
of note who have really existed.

The year after the Baker Street
museum in London opened saw the
Sherlock Holmes Museum at Meiringen
in Switzerland open too. Meiringen is
near to The Reichenbach Falls where
in 1891 Holmes met and defeated his
greatest enemy Professor Moriarty, the

"Napoleon of crime"; it is therefore a kind of Mecca for many Holmesians and the perfect place to open the museum. The museum is located in a totally refurbished English Church and exhibits many donated or loaned items of Holmesian interest, including of course the reconstruction of the famous Baker Street sitting room. A great amount of thought and effort was put into this museum and even the windows were made in London and shipped to Switzerland as well as the wallpaper, which has an authentic 1890s pattern and was also bought and shipped from London. And in case you thought that museums were silent places, the BBC even kindly compiled an hour's worth of accompanying sound effects!

With regard to commemorating and celebrating the mind behind Sherlock Holmes, Conan Doyle doesn't really fair too well considering how much focus Sherlock Holmes receives. Doyle did, however, live and work in Portsmouth on the south coast of England for many years and housed in the Portsmouth City Museum is a permanent private collection of exhibits dedicated to the author himself.

Finally, a little known and interesting fact: Sherlock Holmes is also the only ever fictional character to have a train named after him, when during the 1920s, the London Metropolitan Railway named one of its twenty electric locomotives after him, alongside the likes of fellow non-fictional distinguished Britons, Florence Nightingale, Benjamin Disraeli and Lord Byron.

LEFT Statue of Sherlock Holmes at Meiringen

ABOVE Sign for the Sherlock Holmes Museum at Meiringen in Switzerland

Chapter 6

Sherlock Holmes in the 21ˢᵗ Century

RIGHT Sherlock Holmes statue in Edinburgh

Sherlock Holmes remains a popular figure in the 21st century. One of the reasons that Sherlock Holmes has remained so popular is that he was the first fictional character to popularise the style and methods of detection that he used. Concepts like identifying fingerprints, which have become something everyone knows about, is just one example and that is just one idea that he used out of many. Almost every one of the stories has some type of actual science that was appearing and developing at that time. The fact that we now use these techniques is one of the major reasons that the stories still seem relevant in comparison to so many others with the same history.

Just after the turn of the century Miramax Films produced a made-for-television film in 2002 called *Sherlock: Case of Evil*. With English actor James D'Arcy playing the role of Sherlock Holmes, the film focused on a young Sherlock Holmes in his late twenties. Although Doyle's famous characters are present in the film, such as Professor Moriarty (played by Vincent D'Onofrio), who Holmes shoots before meeting Dr Watson (played by Roger Morlidge), the film plot departs noticeably from the classic depiction, style and backstory of the original material. Once Holmes meets Watson, they embark on investigations into several crime lords, as well as becoming convinced that Holmes didn't finish Moriarty off properly and that he

was still alive and behind an organised drug-dealing ring. The film includes a prostitute (played by Gabriella Anwar) who, posing as a wealthy woman, lures Holmes into the plot. Holmes's brother Mycroft is also in the film (played by Richard E. Grant) and, contrary to his original character, is an opium addict, thanks to the work of Moriarty.

Sherlock: Case of Evil didn't meet with fabulous critical acclaim in fact. The film critic of eFilmCritic only gave it one star out of five, writing: "Let's just accept the idea that Sherlock Holmes needs to be sexed up and made relevant for a twenty-first century audience. Do writer/producer Piers Ashworth and director Graham Theakston manage to make an entertaining movie out of that? No. In their hands, Sherlock becomes a generic hero tortured by the past and Moriarty becomes a thug without any sort of air of mystery about him. ... The two leads, D'Arcy and D'Onofrio, are especially weak. Forget previous portrayals of Holmes and Moriarty, and just focus on their tendency to chew scenery and do little, if anything, with body language."

The Doyle estate tapped British writer Anthony Horowitz (author of the Alex Rider novels, *The Power of Five* and television *Foyle's War*) to write a new Holmes adventure, in the novel, *House of Silk,* which was released in 2012. In 2009, American author Lyndsay Faye released *Dust and Shadow: An Account of the Ripper Killings by Dr John H. Watson*, also with the blessing of the Doyle estate.

There are also the Guy Ritchie movies, starring Robert Downey, Jr. as Sherlock Holmes, which feature a more action-oriented take on Holmes. The first film, *Sherlock Holmes,* was released in 2009. With Jude Law playing Dr. Watson, the famous duo (with the aid of former adversary Irene Adler) embark on investigating a series of murders that are all connected to occult rituals. Again, the villain in the film, Lord Blackwood (played by Mark Strong) has somehow managed to return from the dead after his supposed execution. The film met with mostly positive critical acclaim and Robert Downey, Jr.'s portrayal of Sherlock Holmes won him a Golden Globe Award for Best Actor on a Comedy.

However, not all critics were enamoured by the film's interpretation of the original Holmes stories and film critic and television personality David Stratton wrote of the film, 'The makers of

LEFT Sherlock Holmes pub

this film are mainly interested in action; that, they believe, is all that gets young audiences into cinemas today. They may be right, but they have ridden roughshod over one of literature's greatest creations in the process." He did, however, praise the production design and score.

The sequel to the first Guy Ritchie film, *Sherlock Holmes: A Game of Shadows*, was then released in 2011. Both Robert Downey, Jr. and Jude Law played Holmes and Watson again. This time the film was influenced by Doyle's *The Final Problem*, and although it does not claim to be a strict adaptation, the film does follow the original story. With Jared Harris playing the role of Professor Moriarty and Stephen Fry playing Holmes's brother Mycroft. Commercially the film was a success, grossing over $545 million worldwide. Critically it received moderately positive reviews.

In America and on CBS, *Elementary* was first broadcast in 2012. The series is an American crime drama that presents a contemporary update of Sir Arthur Conan Doyle's famous detective. This version of Holmes, played by Brit Johnny Lee Miller, has been to rehab and shamed out of London. He's now solving crimes in New York City.

Last, but by no means least, there's Steve Moffat and Mark Gatiss's modern take on the story: BBC's *Sherlock*, which has run for three series so far, with a fourth on its way. *Sherlock* is a British television crime drama that presents a contemporary adaptation of Doyle's Sherlock Holmes detective stories. The series was first broadcast in 2010 with a second series in 2012. The most recent third series, broadcast in 2014 has become the most watched drama series in the United Kingdom since 2001. The success of the BBC's take on Sherlock Holmes has been such that it has been sold to more than two hundred different territories across the globe.

Holmes is played by English film, television, theatre and voice actor Benedict Cumberbatch and English actor Martin Freeman plays his faithful companion and friend Dr. Watson. English film, television and theatre actor Rupert Graves plays the part of Detective Inspector Lestrade; Irish film, television and stage actor Andrew Scott plays Holmes's archnemesis Jim Moriarty; Una Stubbs plays Mrs Hudson, Holmes and Watson's landlady; and co-creator Mark Gatiss plays Sherlock's brother, Mycroft.

The series is predominantly filmed in

Cardiff in Wales, but the exterior shots of 221B Baker Street are filmed in North Gower Street in London.

The contemporary setting for *Sherlock* sees Dr. Watson return from military service in Afghanistan and Holmes as a 'consulting detective' who assists the Metropolitan Police Force, primarily working with Detective Inspector Lestrade, in solving a variety of crimes. Of course throughout, a recurring theme is the on-going battle between Holmes and Moriarty.

The creators of *Sherlock* came to the

series, both with experience of using or adapting Victorian literature for television. As well as both of them being *Doctor Who* writers (Gatiss wrote the Dickensian episode *The Unquiet Dead*), Moffat had previously adapted the *Strange Case of Dr. Jekyll and Mr. Hyde* for the 2007 series *Jekyll.*

Gatiss had been a harsh critic of television adaptations of Conan Doyle's stories in the past and had described them as "too reverential and too slow" and being mostly flippant with regard to adhering to the original Doyle literary canon. It could of course be argued that Holmes's use of modern technology, such as using GPS, text, and the internet to help him solve crimes is as guilty of this as the early adaptations from the 1930s and 1940s. Paul McGuigan, director of two *Sherlock* episodes highlights the fact that the modern take on Doyle's character is totally in keeping with the original Holmes and also points out that 'in the books he would use any device possible and he was always in the lab doing experiments. It's just a modern-day version of it. He will use the tools that are available to him today in order to find things out.'

Despite the new series being firmly based in the modern twenty-first-century world, there are also elements to the stories that firmly cement its authenticity and faithfulness to the original texts. The recurrence of Holmes's adversary Moriarty and the fact that the Baker Street address is still firmly in the picture are good examples of this. In the modern *Sherlock*, Watson returns from the war in Afghanistan, yet the original Watson was invalided home after serving in the Second Anglo-Afghan War that took place from 1878 to 1880. Gatiss made the point that 'it is the same war now … the same unwinnable war'. Oh, and what a politically-correct world we do live in now; of course we couldn't have a modern man smoking tobacco, let alone a pipe, so Cumberbatch's Holmes has to be content with sticking multiple nicotine patches to himself instead!

Undoubtedly biased somewhat, but the Head of Drama at BBC Wales, Piers Wenger, described the way the series portrayed Holmes as 'a dynamic superhero in a modern world, an arrogant, genius sleuth driven by a desire to prove himself cleverer than the perpetrator and the police - everyone in fact".

Sherlock has met with highly positive critical reception and many reviews have

LEFT Filming *Sherlock Holmes* in smoggy London

SHERLOCK HOLMES IN THE 21ST CENTURY

commented on the quality of the writing, performances and direction. Tom Sutcliffe for *The Independent* wrote, '*Sherlock* is a triumph, witty and knowing, without ever undercutting the flair and dazzle of the original. It understands that Holmes isn't really about plot but about charisma ... Flagrantly unfaithful to the original in some respects, *Sherlock* is wonderfully loyal to it in every way that matters.' Commenting specifically about the finale of the second series 'The Reichenbach Fall', Sam Wollaston for *The Guardian* praised the series' faithfulness to Conan Doyle, but also said, 'it will wander, taking in mobile phone technology and computer hacking ... But it doesn't feel like cheating; more like an open relationship, agreed by both parties.'

Sherlock has been nominated for numerous awards including Emmy Awards, and the YouTube Audience Award. The series won a BAFTA for Best Drama Series and Freeman won the award for Best Supporting Actor for his role as Dr. Watson; Cumberbatch was also nominated for Best Actor award.

Watch this space for series four!

> " *Sherlock is a triumph, witty and knowing, without ever undercutting the flair and dazzle of the original.* "

Chapter 7

The Sherlock Holmes Canon

Traditionally, the 'canon' of Sherlock Holmes consists of fifty-six short stories and four novels written by Sir Arthur Conan Doyle. In this context, the term 'canon' is an attempt to distinguish between Conan Doyle's original works and subsequent works by other authors using the same characters.

NOVELS

Here are the four novels of the canon:

1. ***A Study in Scarlet***
   (published in 1887)

2. ***The Sign of the Four***
   (published in 1890)

3. ***The Hound of the Baskervilles***
   (serialised 1901-1902 in *The Strand*)

4. ***The Valley of Fear***
   (serialised 1914-1915)

SHORT STORIES

The fifty-six short stories are compiled in five books:

1. ***The Adventures of Sherlock Holmes***
   (published in 1892)

2. ***The Memoirs of Sherlock Holmes***
   (published in 1894)

3. ***The Return of Sherlock Holmes***
   (published in 1905)

4. ***His Last Bow*** (published in 1917)

5. *The Case-Book of Sherlock Holmes*
   (published in 1927)

Frequently, *The Adventure of ...* is dropped from some story titles in current-day anthologies. However, in their original appearance in *The Strand*, this following is how the titles were given in many cases.

The Adventures of Sherlock Holmes
Published 31st October 1892; contains 12 stories published in *The Strand* between July 1891 and June 1892 with original illustrations by Sidney Paget:

- *A Scandal in Bohemia*
- *The Adventure of the Red-Headed League*
- *A Case of Identity*
- *The Boscombe Valley Mystery*
- *The Five Orange Pips*
- *The Man with the Twisted Lip*
- *The Adventure of the Blue Carbuncle*
- *The Adventure of the Speckled Band*
- *The Adventure of the Engineer's Thumb*
- *The Adventure of the Noble Bachelor*
- *The Adventure of the Beryl Coronet*
- *The Adventure of the Copper Beeches*

THE SHERLOCK HOLMES CANON

The Memoirs of Sherlock Holmes

Contains 12 stories published in *The Strand* as further episodes of the *Adventures* between December 1892 and December 1893 with original illustrations by Sidney Paget:

- *Silver Blaze*
- *The Adventure of the Cardboard Box*
  (this story is included as part of *His Last Bow* in lifetime editions of the collection)
- *The Adventure of the Yellow Face*
- *The Adventure of the Stockbroker's Clerk*
- *The Adventure of the Gloria Scott*
  (Holmes's first case, described to Watson)
- *The Adventure of the Musgrave Ritual*
  (another early case, told by Holmes to Watson)
- *The Adventure of the Reigate Squire*
- *The Adventure of the Crooked Man*
- *The Adventure of the Resident Patient*
- *The Adventure of the Greek Interpreter*
  (Mycroft appears for the first time)
- *The Adventure of the Naval Treaty*
- *The Final Problem* (Watson reports the death of Holmes)

The Return of Sherlock Holmes

Contains 13 stories published in *The Strand* between October 1903 and December 1904 with original illustrations by Sidney Paget:

- *The Adventure of the Empty House*
  (the return of Holmes)
- *The Adventure of the Norwood Builder*
- *The Adventure of the Dancing Men*
- *The Adventure of the Solitary Cyclist*
- *The Adventure of the Priory School*
- *The Adventure of Black Peter*
- *The Adventure of Charles Augustus Milverton*
- *The Adventure of the Six Napoleons*
- *The Adventure of the Three Students*
- *The Adventure of the Golden Pince-Nez*
- *The Adventure of the Missing Three-Quarter*
- *The Adventure of the Abbey Grange*
- *The Adventure of the Second Stain*

His Last Bow

Contains seven stories published between 1908 and 1917. (American editions often have *The Adventure of the Cardboard Box* in this collection instead of in *The Memoirs of Sherlock Holmes*.):

- ***The Adventure of Wisteria Lodge***
(originally published simply as *A Reminiscence of Mr. Sherlock Holmes*, this story is made up of two parts given separate titles: *The Singular Experience of Mr. John Scott Eccles* and *The Tiger of San Pedro*)
- ***The Adventure of the Red Circle***
- ***The Adventure of the Bruce-Partington Plans*** (Mycroft appears)
- ***The Adventure of the Dying Detective***
- ***The Disappearance of Lady Frances Carfax***
- ***The Adventure of the Devil's Foot***
- ***His Last Bow*** (told in third-person)

The Case-Book of Sherlock Holmes
Contains 12 stories published between 1921 and 1927:

- ***The Adventure of the Mazarin Stone*** *(told in the third-person)*
- ***The Problem of Thor Bridge***
- ***The Adventure of the Creeping Man***
- ***The Adventure of the Sussex Vampire***
- ***The Adventure of the Three Garridebs***
- ***The Adventure of the Illustrious Client***
- ***The Adventure of the Three Gables***

"It was a nice equipment for a respectable citizen"
The Bruce Partington Plans

- ***The Adventure of the Blanched Soldier** (narrated by Holmes; Watson does not appear)*
- ***The Adventure of the Lion's Mane** (narrated by Holmes; Watson does not appear)*
- ***The Adventure of the Retired Colourman***
- ***The Adventure of the Veiled Lodger***
- ***The Adventure of Shoscombe Old Place***

In addition to the 'canon' Conan Doyle wrote (occasionally with a co-writer) there are a number of vignettes, play adaptations and essays involving Holmes (some already discussed), and two short stories in which Holmes makes a possible cameo appearance. Most were published in various places during his lifetime; another has only come to light since his death. These are listed below with further detail.

SHORT STORIES

The Field Bazaar (1896)

The Field Bazaar was written during an Edinburgh University fundraising event. Doyle had been requested by his university to contribute a short piece of literature for a charity magazine. In the story, Watson has received a similar request and whilst he reads the letter at breakfast, Holmes correctly deduces the sender of the letter and Watson's thoughts with regard to the letter. It shares many similarities to the canonical stories. Aside from the metafictional twist in which Watson supplants Doyle as the author publishing his own stories in a magazine, it also plays not only on the famous skill of Holmes' observations producing apparently miraculous results, but also upon the notion of the 'traditional breakfast scenes', which open many Holmes short stories.

The Lost Special (1898)

Though Doyle had killed off his character by 1894, he still wrote other short stories for publication in *The Strand Magazine*. *The Lost Special* was one such story, a seemingly inexplicable mystery in which a special train and its few passengers disappear between two stations. After the mystery is described in full, it is stated that a letter appeared in the press, giving a proposed solution from an amateur reasoner of some celebrity. It is possible, and has been proposed by Haining, Tracy and Green amongst others, that this 'amateur reasoner' was Sherlock Holmes. The strongest clue to this is the quote "once one has eliminated the impossible ..." used by Holmes throughout his deductions. However, this suggested solution is proved wrong by a confession from the organising criminal once he is later arrested for an unrelated crime. It is suggested by Haining that Doyle was 'getting out some Holmes' during the series hiatus, but given the failure of the unnamed detective it appears he was parodying his most famous creation. The story was published in book form in Arthur Conan Doyle's *Tales of Terror and Mystery* in 1923 and has appeared in French editions of the complete adventures for many years.

The Man with the Watches (1898)

Like *The Lost Special*, *The Man with the Watches* appeared in *The Strand* (in 1898), and later in *Round the Fire Stories* and *Tales of Terror and Mystery*. It follows the same pattern, the mystery this time surrounding the appearance of a dead man in a railway carriage, with six pocket watches in his jacket. An explanation is offered by an amateur detective, but the narrator notes it to be flawed, as it doesn't take into account all the facts. A man involved in the accidental murder of the victim writes a letter to the detective, saying that it was a "mighty clever solution"

but entirely incorrect and continues to share the true events of that day. It shares the same backing for categorising as the Sherlock Holmes story *The Lost Special*, and appears in French anthologies. The story was adapted for BBC Radio 4 in 2009 as *The Thirteen Watches*, in an episode from *The Further Adventures of Sherlock Holmes*. The number of watches was changed because the new title came from a reference (in the Holmes story *The Noble Bachelor*) to Holmes' involvement with the watches incident.

Plot for Sherlock Holmes Story (c.1900)

When searching through Conan Doyle's papers, Hesketh Pearson, a biographer of his, came across a plan for an unwritten story. As Richard Lancelyn Green notes, "there is no evidence to show that it is by [Conan Doyle] and strong internal evidence to suggest that it's not". Various authors have attempted to complete the story (named *The Adventure of the Tall Man* by Peter Haining) and put it alongside the canon. Some are very close to Doyle's plot, others include variations. However, no 'official' completion has been made (in the same way as *The Exploits of Sherlock Holmes* was intended as an official continuation of the canon).

How Watson Learned the Trick (1924)

In 1924, several authors were approached to contribute to the library of Queen Mary's Dolls' House. Conan Doyle wrote a short Sherlock Holmes story, just 503 words long, onto the tiny pages of a specially constructed miniature book: *How Watson Learned the Trick*. The story was later published alongside works by other authors in *The Book of the Queen's Dolls' House Library*. Though written 28 years after *The Field Bazaar*, this is almost a companion piece to that story. Like The *Field Bazaar*, this story is a breakfast scene, during which Watson attempts to mimic Holmes's style in guessing his thoughts. Watson's intuitions are proved wrong however. Unlike almost all parts of the Sherlock Holmes story, it is written in the third person, presumably due to its length.

SHERLOCK HOLMES ON STAGE

Angels of Darkness (c. 1889)

Unpublished until 2000, this play was written shortly after *A Study in Scarlet* was published. It is essentially a rewrite of the American chapters of *A Study in Scarlet*, with the London action moving to San Francisco. Holmes is not present, but Watson is, in a very different form. He acts discreditably, and even marries another woman. The publication of this play was at first suppressed, Doyle's biographer, John Dickson Carr stated that it would do no good for the public to read this, a view that Haining endorses readily. The play is notable for its contrasting sensationalist and comic scenes. It is contained in Klinger's Apocrypha.

Sherlock Holmes: A Drama in Four Acts (or Sherlock Holmes, 1899)

The original Sherlock Holmes play, written by Arthur Conan Doyle and William Gillette, had a successful run of over thirty years. It has many original parts, which are not found in the short stories, but borrows many events from the canonical adventures, namely *A Scandal in Bohemia* and *The Final Problem*. Also, it has elements from *A Study in Scarlet*, *The Sign of Four*, *The Boscombe Valley Mystery*, *The Adventure of the Greek Interpreter*, and *The Adventure of the Naval Treaty*. It includes the very first mention of the phrase "Elementary, my dear Watson." While Conan Doyle wrote the original version, it is unclear how much of his material survived in the play as performed, which was written by Gillette. Conan Doyle and Gillette later revised the play together; it has since been revised twice by others.

The Speckled Band (or The Stonor Case, 1902)

Around 1902, Doyle wrote and produced a play based on his short story *The Adventure of the Speckled Band*. It premièred eight years later at the Adelphi Theatre in London on 4th June 1910 with H. A. Saintsbury as Sherlock Holmes and Lyn Harding as Dr. Grimesby Roylott. The play, originally entitled *The Stonor Case*, differs from the story in several small details, such as the names of some of the characters.

The Crown Diamond: An Evening With Mr Sherlock Holmes (1921)

The Crown Diamond is an alternate version of the short story *The Adventure of the Mazarin Stone*, though it predates its counterpart by some time. At some point during the original run, the short story was adapted from the play. This is the reason that the narrative is told in third person rather than by the traditional narrator Watson. Some claim that the play originally appeared in an early draft of *Sherlock Holmes* (above) and was later removed, with some elements finding their way into *The Adventure of the Empty House* before the entire play was resurrected, some years later, into *The Crown Diamond* and *The Mazarin Stone*.

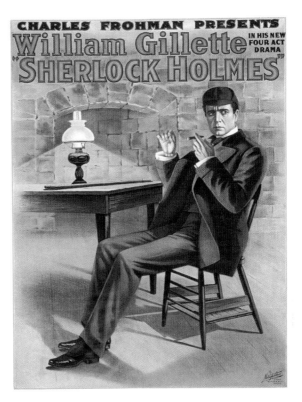

ABOVE Charles Frohman presents William Gillette in his new four act drama, *Sherlock Holmes*

Design & Artwork: ALEX YOUNG

Published by: DEMAND MEDIA LIMITED

Publisher: JASON FENWICK

Written by: MICHELLE BRACHET